FACEPLATE TURNING
Features • Projects • Practice

The best from WOODTURNING magazine

FACEPLATE TURNING
Features • Projects • Practice

The best from WOODTURNING magazine

GUILD OF MASTER CRAFTSMAN PUBLICATIONS LTD

This collection first published in 1996 by
Guild of Master Craftsman Publications Ltd,
Castle Place, 166 High Street, Lewes,
East Sussex BN7 1XU

© GMC Publications Ltd 1996

ISBN 0 946819 99 8

Printed and bound in Great Britain by the University Press,
Cambridge

Cover photograph supplied by Jules Tattersall

Contents

Notes

Please note that names, addresses, prices etc. were correct at the time the articles were originally published, but may since have changed.

MEASUREMENTS: Cautionary Note

Throughout the book instances will be found where a metric measurement has fractionally varying imperial equivalents, usually within 1/16in either way. This is because in each particular case the closest imperial equivalent has been given. For this reason it is recommended, particularly on the smaller projects, that a drawing is made of the work to ensure that the measurements have not lost anything in translation.

Also, although the measurements given here are carefully calculated and are accurate, some variation may occur when pieces are hand turned, so care must be taken and adjustment may be necessary as the work progresses.

A mixture of metric and imperial measurements should NEVER be used – always use either one or the other.

Introduction

Ever since its first publication in 1990, *Woodturning* magazine has covered the whole range of woodturning subjects: between centres turning (spindle), ornamental turning, faceplate work, along with tool developments, new lathes, new techniques, traditional techniques, green wood turning, decorating turnings with carving and colour, and so on.

This book is compiled from issues of *Woodturning* published from 1990 to mid-1995, and covers some of the new forms of faceplate turning, as well as traditional styles and techniques. There are features on turners, who describe their work and how and why they have developed the way they have; projects, which show exactly how to produce items, and technical articles which explain particular methods of working that can be applied to your own projects.

Although bowls, plates, cups, vases, goblets, pots, vessels, and some turned sculptures, are all covered under the term faceplate turning, turners themselves know that faceplates are rarely used for holding work on the lathe nowadays – a variety of chucks have taken over their role. The common feature of these objects is that they are hollowed and, because of this, they would be difficult or impossible to produce between centres (spindle turning).

Faceplate turning has seen some dramatic developments in recent years. From simple bowls and platters, turners have moved on to natural edged bowls, hollow forms large and small, translucent thin vessels, sculptures and so on. Faceplate turners are redefining the limits of the craft.

The aims of this book are to allow those new to *Woodturning* magazine to see the best of what has already been published, and to draw together articles for those turners whose main interest is in faceplate work. It also gives long-time readers a chance to replace those features which they may have lost, as some back issues of *Woodturning* have sold out.

I hope you enjoy reading about the work of these turners and will find the projects and techniques useful.

Neil Bell
Editor, *Woodturning*

Dennis Elliott was born in London, England, in 1950. He married his American wife Iona in 1972 and has been a resident of the US (currently living in Sherman, Connecticut) since 1975. He is both a musician and woodturner by profession.

Dennis started turning wood in 1972 and is basically self taught. For the last few years he has been concentrating mainly on large burlwood vessels and wall sculptures with frequent use of sandblasting and carving techniques. His works can be found in major corporate and private collections.

Among the awards he has received are 'Honoraria' Texas Fine Arts Association's New American Talent 1988; 'Award of Distinction' The Pennsylvania State University, Crafts 22; 'Best in Wood Award' The Octagon Center for the Arts, Ames, Iowa 1989; and 'Certificate of Excellence in Wood' Art Horizons — a leading International Art Competition, New York.

He is co-founder of the Nutmeg Woodturners' League, a founding member of the American Association of Woodturners, a member of The Association of Woodturners of Great Britain and an international member of The Guild of Master Craftsmen.

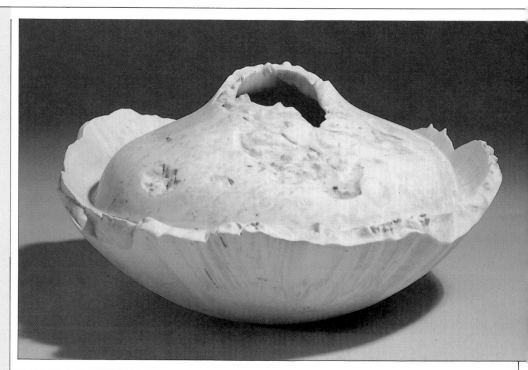

Making a
Hollow Vessel

DENNIS ELLIOTT

For your benefit, the author retraces the steps he took when turning a piece that has aroused interest ever since.

When my wife, who is also my business manager, informed me that some weeks ago she had sent slides of my work to a new magazine in England devoted entirely to woodturning and that she had just heard back that, not only did they like the slides, but would like me to write about the making of one particular piece, I was joyful! Just to think that I might have something published in a brand new mag in my old HOMELAND, THE UK! My Dad will be proud! 'What piece?' I asked. 'Guess,' she said. 'Don't tell me it's the hollow form with the very level natural rim, almost flat top and silly little hole from which I hollowed it?' 'Yes,' she said. 'I asked you not to tell me that,' I replied.

What is it with this piece? The day I made it I must have been crazy and vowed never to do anything like it again. You see, it's not that it's just a hollow form, which is hard enough anyway, but with this particular piece I had created an almost flat top, with an opening so small that I could barely get a tool in it, let alone wiggle it about to get the inside out.

Stewart Hooker

Oh well, I did manage to hollow it with the use of a Stewart Hooker so I'll try to retrace the steps and see what happens.

The first step with this type of work is to locate a suitable piece of burl (or burr, as it's called in the UK), in this case maple. Having just received a shipment of 800lb of wood, I was optimistic that I'd have no trouble finding the right piece.

What I'm looking for is something that will yield a basic open bowl shape, with a relatively flat or even rim, that will surround an enclosed form. This is not easy to find as there is usually some undulation of burl surfaces. I find the best way to check for this is with some type of tube resting on the domed surface and seeing where it touches and where it doesn't. (Photo 1.)

The piece shown would only yield the more typical up and down movements of the rim, which is a shame because I feel the level rim on the original piece holds the key to its success. These are one of a kind objects and it's hard to duplicate. After repeating this process, checking my entire hoard of wood and finding nothing better, I'll go ahead and make this piece since the procedure is the same anyway.

Having decided where the rim will be I mark out the circle using a compass and chalk. (Photo 2.) This also gives me my

centre point. (Photo 3.) I then cut out this circle on the bandsaw. (Photo 3.) This can be a wasteful procedure but I am eliminating a defect on the underside, so it's not as bad as it looks.

I start the majority of my work between centres as it gives me the opportunity to adjust the alignment for the best effect. (Photo 4.)

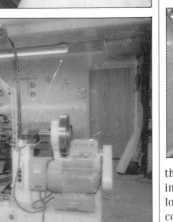

The underside of the bowl is roughed out (Photo 5) and the base made flat or slightly concave (Photo 6). I can then

mount a faceplate accurately, using a threaded mandrel and pin; the pin locates in the hole left by the tailstock. (Photos 7 and 8.) I then complete nine-

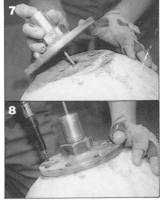

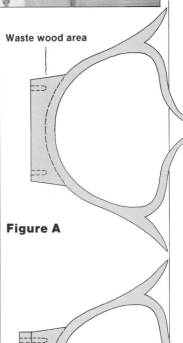

tenths of the outside shape. (Photo 9.) I can't do the entire outside as I now have screws in the base, so I'll plan my design to disappear under the points of the screws at this stage, knowing that the area with screw holes will be removed, and the outside completed, when I reverse turn the piece at the final stage. If this all sounds confusing, Figure A should clarify what I'm going for.

I then work from the front and define the rim. (Photo 10.) I

then shape the outside of the internal form and what I'm looking for is the two shapes to come together at the rim and blend together into one integral shape.

Sandblasts

When I'm happy with the overall effect, I take the bowl outside and sandblast all the natural surfaces clean. This lets me see what the opening will look like: when it's back on the lathe, I can make any adjustments with a sharp turning tool. Not that the tool will stay sharp for long — after sandblasting, one or two seconds and it's dull! I could sandblast it after the piece is hollowed, but trying to

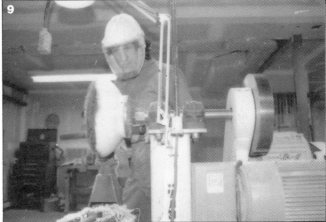

Waste wood area

Figure A

Figure B

remove silica sand from inside a damp hollow form is . . . well, trying!

Next stage is to bore the piece to final depth. For this, I use a 25mm 1″ bit in the tailstock (Photo 11) and then start

hollowing out the interior. For this I use two tools, one is basically a long handle, with a small toolbit clamped in the end, that can be swivelled to help go round the inside (made by Jim Thompson*) (Photo 12) and, where that can't reach, I use a Stewart Hooker, which has a built in caliper that can help you judge the wall thickness (Photo 13). It's quite a long

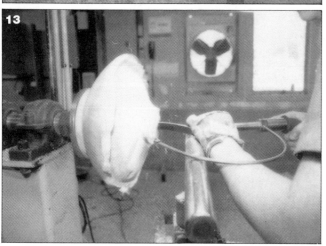

process that involves continually stopping the lathe and blowing or digging out the shavings. Since they can't escape otherwise, they would eventually build up and start to grab hold of the shank of the tool. I like to stop the cut before that happens.

Once the piece is hollowed out to my satisfaction, and that means an even wall thickness and a good finish from the tools, it's time to sand the outside. For this I'll use 50mm 2″ velcro backed sanding discs, held in a small anglehead air tool, starting at 180 thru to 400 grit. (Photo 14.)

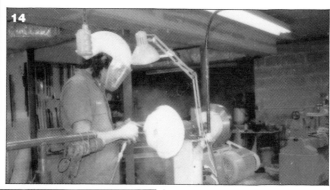

made internal cone chuck (Photo 15) that the neck of the

Now it's time to reverse turn the piece and take out those screw holes.

Once the faceplate is removed, I can see six screw holes and one depression in the centre that was made at its very first mounting on the lathe . . . between centres. It's a very important centre point that's been there all along and I've used it to locate the faceplate accurately and, now, to take care of the base.

Cone Chuck

This piece being basically a hollow form, I'll use a home

piece will fit in. It must be deep enough so that the natural opening does not touch the bottom of it and it just touches the piece on its shoulder. I then slide up the tailstock back into its original hole (Photo 16), tap

it into alignment, and then turn off the base along with the screw holes and complete the outside shape. (Photo 17.) Because the mark from the tailcentre is now standing proud of the base, a little handwork will remove it quite easily. However, I usually leave it there until the piece is dry so I can put it back on the lathe to true up the base, which will have become uneven during the drying process.

Most of my work is finished with a penetrating tung oil finish. ∎

* Jim Thompson — tool maker and lathe maker, 1021 Miller Road, Greenville, South Carolina 29607, USA (803) 288-1309.

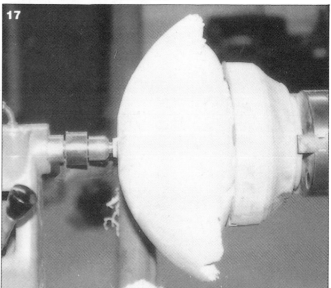

TURN A TABLE

JUDD MOSSER

Turned parts are included in Judd Mosser's furniture designs because they yield a light, yet strong, form. Here he describes how to turn an unusual table from sugar maple gall. This table, called Apperception, was featured in the National Furniture Invitational XII Exhibition in Cleveland, Ohio.

Photos 9 and 10 The finished table, sugar maple and black walnut 1015mm 40" H x 1395mm 55" W x 610mm 24" DIA.

Born in Lakewood, Ohio in 1951, Judd Mosser spent his early years on a family farm near Cleveland. Later his family moved to a small town near Buffalo, New York, where he now lives with his wife, Denise, and two young daughters.

He attended the University of Vermont and lived in the Green Mountain state for a number of years.

It was there he began turning as a vocation. Small cherry wood items such as spoons, finely-turned honeyspoons with octagonal handles, and candle holders were his mainstay, which he produced by the thousand.

He recently bought a 40-year-old large pattern makers' lathe with heavy castings.

Earlier this year he replaced the 50mm 2" shaft and babbitt bearings with a 55mm 2¼" shaft and double-row tapered roller bearings and raised the shaft height 125mm 5" giving it a swing of 760mm 30" over the bed.

Its combination of weight and slow speed (80-900 RPM) has given him the opportunity to work large, unbalanced pieces of wood and to further explore the turned form in his furniture designs.

everal years ago I began turning furniture pieces. By that I mean tables and pedestals in which the main part of the design has been turned. The pieces evolve slowly, partly because the green turnings need to dry before I re-turn them as furniture.

My basement studio contains lots of these turnings in some stage of drying. I include turned parts into my furniture designs partly because turning yields a light, yet strong, form.

This physical aspect enables me to create interesting visual forms I have only begun to explore. Methods of joinery, from the turned elements to the other parts of the designs, I also find intriguing.

Work began on *Apperception*, the table shown here, in 1991. I had worked with sugar maple galls before, liking the dark and medium brown colours to be found beneath the bark.

Because galls are caused by damage to a tree, either by insects or the constant rubbing of one tree against another, the tree is often dead or decaying.

So, spalting, worm holes and cracks blackened by rainwater can be expected, plus the unusual growth patterns formed as the tree attempts in vain to heal itself.

The gall for *Apperception* came from a large tree cut for lumber. Loggers consider a gall a defect, commonly cutting out that portion of the log and leaving it lying in the forest.

Bowl table

After some thought, I decided to turn a table with a bowl in its form. Early work with a chainsaw was needed to hew out a semblance of that form, then, with help, I manoeuvred it into my basement studio for its initial turning.

Although the faceplate on the outboard side of my lathe is 305mm 12" in diameter, I have a wooden faceplate of 915mm 36" DIA that can be bolted to it (Photo 1).

This is sturdy and adds a lot of stability and safety when turning bigger pieces of wood.

The wooden faceplate also allows me to easily drill holes and screw lag bolts through it, to attach the work when necessary. This is especially important whenever I have to attach an off-centre piece of work.

In this case, I did not have a flat base on my workpiece to attach to the faceplate. Therefore, I joined two 75mm 3" x 140mm 5½" x 405mm 16" blocks of wood to the faceplate and attached my work to the blocks (Photo 2).

I normally use 8mm 5/16" DIA lag bolts of various lengths with a small washer and always place them in an area of the work to be removed after turning is completed.

Care must be taken to countersink the bolt heads and small washers deep enough to prevent them contacting tools during turning. Checking them periodically is a must, as a chance metal-to-metal encounter can cause problems rather quickly.

Once secured, I normally run the lathe for several minutes, while standing clear, to be sure everything is holding.

I turned *Apperception* at 80 RPM to reduce the

Photo 1 A wooden faceplate of 915mm 36" DIA is bolted to my lathe.

Photo 2 Two blocks of wood were fixed to the faceplate and the work attached to them.

unbalanced centrifugal force caused by the bowl not being centred in the table. This slow speed means there is little chance of the piece flying off the lathe.

I checked for any loosening of the piece each time the lathe was turned off. I turned this piece over four days without incident.

I used either a roughing gouge, a bowl gouge that I modified to more closely resemble a scraper, or a 12mm ½" round-nose scraper. (Photos 3 and 4).

I first turned it to a uniform thickness of 55mm 2¼". I knew how much sugar maple can move and warp during the drying process, and was determined to have as much wood as possible when it came time to true up the piece after it was dry.

After the initial turning, it measured 1525mm 60" in length with a bowl of 610mm 24" DIA, and weighed 68lbs.

Because drying wood is a complex subject with numerous methods and as many results, I knew I would need to use caution in drying this piece. Sugar maple of this thickness is prone to splitting until it is safely below its free moisture content.

After that, it can warp considerably until it is quite dry. I carefully sealed, with several coats of varnish, all the end grain and any other areas that experience had shown to be vulnerable to splitting.

Plastic bags

I then placed two clear plastic rubbish bags over the piece and taped them together. I use clear bags because, after a day or two, condensation forms and can be seen on the inside of the bag. This tells me that it is time to open it for a few hours.

I repeat this process many times, over some months, until the condensation takes much longer to form and the piece can safely be left out of the bag for long periods. Eventually the bag is removed permanently.

One year later the piece had lost 21lbs, the equivalent of 2½ gallons of water.

I use my basement for drying wood up to this point, as it gives a fairly constant temperature and relative humidity readings.

When the piece was no longer losing weight in this environment, I placed it in a specially-heated room where it lost another 3lbs over several months, reaching a final moisture content of about 8%.

Now the final turning could begin. I use a chain hoist when mounting larger work on the lathe (Photo 5) as it gives extra safety and precise positioning and is infinitely easier on my back.

Turning a piece such as this is hazardous, as decaying wood can be unpredictable. Splinters of any size can break off at any time and be pushed along the tool directly onto your hand. Because of this, I always wear a glove.

The biggest hazard lies in not holding a steady tool and not concentrating for the required hours on end on what the tool is doing in the mesmerising blur of wood.

To turn the bottom side of the table, I continued to use the blocks of wood holding the work away from the faceplate ▶

Rite of Passage, spalted maple 180mm 7" H x 280mm 11" DIA.

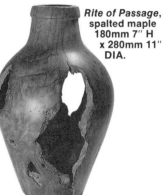

Spirit Water Vessel, sugar maple gall 355mm 14" H x 230mm 9" DIA.

Willow vessel 240mm 9½" H x 280mm 11" DIA.

Photos 3 and 4 At work with roughing gouge and scraper.

Photo 5 A chain hoist helps when mounting work on the lathe.

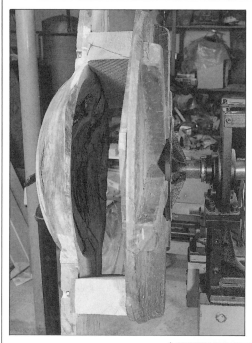

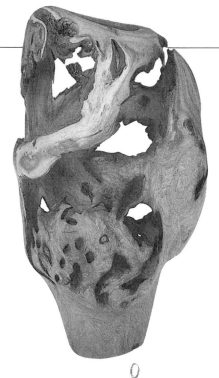

The Wind, a Woman and Child, mesquite burl 405mm 16″ H x 230mm 9″ W x 180mm 7″ DIA.

Red oak leaf 135mm 5¼″ H x 90mm 3½″ W x 135mm 5¼″ DIA.

Photos 6 and 7 The wooden blocks hold the work away from the faceplate when turning the bottom side of the table.

(Photos 6 and 7) as this allowed me access to the inside of the bowl for measurement of the bowl thickness.

When working on bigger pieces, I always allow more time because of the larger surface areas to be worked. I think that whenever the diameter of a piece is doubled, the actual surface area to be worked increases by a factor of four.

Because this piece could not be sanded while spinning on the lathe, I made sure the final cuts were as smooth as possible (Photo 8). Final sanding was done with a random orbital sander and a hand block.

Once removed from the lathe, the table edges were cut with a hand-held circular saw guided by a 1219mm 4′ long metal ruler clamped to the table top.

The piece was finished with four or five coats of polymerised tung oil. The legs were made from black walnut which I darkened with pigment to emulate the dark brown hue of the maple gall. They were joined with blind mortise and tenon joints and finished with three or four coats of varnish (Photos 9 and 10).

Other examples of my work are found on these pages. ■

Red oak and brass octagonal lamp 392mm 15½″ H (base) x 200mm 8″ W x 200mm 8″ DIA.

Voice of My Past, manzanita root burl 610mm 24″ x 200mm 8″ DIA.

Photo 8 The final cuts were made as smooth as possible.

When John Fox met three turners from different countries at the World Woodturning Conference in Delaware, he hit upon the idea of a common project to cement their friendship.

Three of a kind

JOHN FOX

John Fox was born in San Diego, California, and later studied Communication at the university there. After graduating, he became the first person from his home town to go to study in Fukui, its sister city in Japan.

There he learnt to speak Japanese and pursued his interest in Japanese design and architecture. A special focus of his was the traditional lacquer ware industry, in which, he says, craftsmanship and design are unequalled.

This effort led to friendships and to individual tuition in turning for eight months.

On a trip home to California, John went to one of the Challenge series of exhibitions in Los Angeles, and that night called Albert LeCoff at the Wood Turning Center in Philadelphia, Pennsylvania. He has been hooked on woodturning ever since.

His achievements have included presenting at the World Turning Conference, coming up with the *Child's Play* project featured here, reviewing the *Challenge V* exhibition for the World Turning Center, and sending boxes made by Vic Wood and Hans Weissflog to Japan for lacquer treatment (both were bought at the Challenge V auction).

Last summer was spent at Harvard's Graduate School of Design studying architecture. John plans to apply for graduate studies in this field as well as human factors/ergonomics.

As graduate school doesn't start until the autumn, he is seeking a job in the design field, feeling a career in this would be ideal for him.

The project was simple – to send three marbles to three turners in three countries, give them the same basic guidelines and then compare the different designs they sent me in a magazine article or an exhibition.

I'd met the three men at the 1993 World Woodturning Conference in Delaware, and created the project to build on these international friendships and to bring turning to the public's attention, hopefully encouraging people to take it up.

One of the three, Stephen Hughes lives in Australia, another, Siegfried Schreiber, in Germany, while the third, Soren Berger, is from New Zealand.

The challenge I set them was to incorporate three marbles into a turned form so the marbles

▶

'After seeing his flawless work, I wrote to congratulate him, describing it as a classic example of German engineering.'

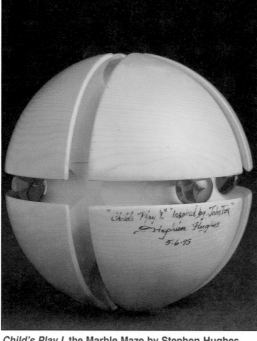

Child's Play I, the Marble Maze by Stephen Hughes.

Child's Play II, by Siegfried Schreiber.

could be moved but not removed. The aim was to cause someone to say, "How did he do that?" when looking at or playing with the finished item.

I called the project *Child's Play* for two reasons: first, the object to be made was something to play with and, second, it was a play on words, the technical skills needed to make it being beyond a child's ability.

The wood could be of the turner's own choice, the finish had to be natural, the edges and corners rounded, the size and shape of the piece also up to the turner. The three finished pieces, along with sketches and notes, were to be sent to me in Japan.

If all three arrived in time, I planned to submit them to the *Challenge V* travelling exhibition, which would have been ideal for the exposure and educational part of the project.

But it was important each man moved at his own pace. As it turned out, one piece arrived within a month, another in six months, and the

Child's Play III, by Soren Berger.

third, in about 18 months.

So I wasn't able to give the project public exposure at *Challenge V,* as it wasn't complete. Still, not all projects are ready on time – if ever.

Stephen Hughes, from Victoria, tells me his piece, *Marble Maze I,* was completed six hours after he made a sketch. His work has pointed edges where the cuts cross over, but he says this is needed to keep the three marbles intact. Too wide an opening would have resulted, had the corners been rounded back.

Stephen adds that his puzzle is 'extremely difficult' to crack, the three marbles having to be lodged in the centre of the sphere at the same time.

Made from huon pine, a wood which marks easily, his work has a light, clear nitrocellulose coating to prevent soiling.

The project has since inspired Stephen to develop the idea of making a series of *Marble Mazes,* possibly in other mediums, such as cast plastics, as well as wood.

'The challenge I set them was to incorporate three marbles into a turned form so the marbles could be moved but not removed.'

He thinks they would have an international appeal and is looking at the possibility of giving the designs to a company on a royalty basis.

Siegfried Schreiber, from Vaihingen-Ensingen, has made *Child's Play II* from pear wood, treated with oil. It has no fixed base. Not only the marbles move about in the object but the object itself moves around.

After seeing his flawless work, I wrote to congratulate him, describing it as 'a classic example of German engineering, instantly recognizable as one of his pieces'.

At first glance, the work seems quite simple, though the beauty is instantly apparent. But on closer inspection and handling, you can appreciate the subtle lines and edges.

After rotating clockwise and counter-clockwise with one, two or three marbles, the engineering aspects come to life. It is a toy, but one which teaches, a work of art yet something meant to be touched. It embodies what I had envisioned from the start of the project.

The pear wood is gorgeous, as the reflective nature of the grain gives a sense of depth. Before it arrived, I had never seen or touched this type of wood before.

MARBLES

Child's Play III, from Swedish-born Soren Berger, in Christchurch, is also beautifully made, consisting of marbles spinning between two clear plastic domes. There is a lid to cover the piece when it isn't in use.

Soren says that to start with he planned the marbles to be contained by the wood in the structure of the piece. But the more he worked on this idea, it became evident that the greatest fascination was created when you could see the marbles moving.

The idea of a dome started to form, and with the aid of the vacuum chuck he uses in his turning, he made a series of different sized domes, thinking that with these the marbles could be contained yet still visible.

Things were still not very exciting, Soren tells me, until, by accident, he ended up with the marbles sandwiched between two domes of different size. This created an interesting illusion and a fascinating effect with the marbles.

The lid gives an element of surprise when the viewer removes it, while the cherry wood can be touched and admired from all sides.

I hope these three projects will help non-turners appreciate the time, effort and planning behind every great piece – to realise that turnings do not appear out of thin air, but are the culmination of a series of steps and decisions calling for careful thought and consideration. ●

Hugh Foster was born in Kansas and raised in suburban Chicago. He received a BA from Carthage College in 1966 and has been teaching English at Lincoln High School, Manitowoc, Wisconsin, ever since. Hugh has been a woodworking hobbyist since 1967 and a woodworking author since 1984. He has had some 200 articles, reviews, project plans, tool manuals and books published since he took up the pen. Currently available worldwide is his *Biscuit Joiner Handbook*, published by Sterling in the US and Cassell in the UK. He has become increasingly interested in turning and hopes to be a regular contributor to *Woodturning* for the foreseeable future. Come in Hugh.

MOULTHROP ON TURNING

HUGH FOSTER

Photographs by Ed Moulthrop

One of the impressive sights at the Loughborough International Seminar in September 1991 was that of Ed Moulthrop demonstrating the techniques, lathe and tools he uses to create his massive masterpieces. If you were not fortunate enough to be there, this article will give you a taste of what it was like to attend one of his workshops.

One of the crucial differences, perhaps, between artist and craftsman, at least in woodworking, is that the artists often appears to be building **some**thing from **no**thing.

This definition surely establishes Ed Moulthrop as one of the premier artists of our day: He made his own lathe with parts from the junk yard; no one else had yet produced a lathe on which Moulthrop could turn the vessels that he imagined. He still smiths his own tools in his back yard (though Dale Nish's Craft Supplies USA has just begun to cast copies of Moulthrop's tools. He turns his masterpieces not from exotic species torn from the Amazon rainforests, but instead from local, even common southern woods.

A vivid Romantic imagination helps to name the woods. Tulip poplar, called poplar, used only as a secondary material by furnituremakers, becomes Tulipwood, an exotic sounding treasure. Were he making junk projects, we'd say, 'Behave yourself'. Instead, we admire the work — all aspects of it — and we hope to learn enough from it to help us to become better craftsmen. Artists are apparently born, not made, but looking at Moulthrop's way of working may improve the ways we plan and execute our shop tasks.

Atlanta Tree-Cutters

Moulthrop's planning begins at the material gathering stage. Because his materials aren't commercially available, he has trained several Atlanta area tree-cutters exactly what to look for in type of wood, figure, size, etc., and what he definitely doesn't want. They notify him

of a good find — perhaps one section of log from each 1000 trees they cut. The logs are carefully stored, wet enough to prevent the cracking and checking that air-drying too often causes, until their day at the lathe arrives. Moulthrop has found the answer to the question: What material should I work in? Ours too should most likely be both local and relatively inexpensive, but nevertheless interesting and beautiful.

1. The green log. 760mm 30" diam. x 1170mm 46" high. Log section 1300 lbs. Mounting the faceplate

The accompanying photos, all by the artist, and all captioned by the artist, show him working a 1300 pound log. A lathe that will turn such a huge chunk of wood must be a special tool indeed. Moulthrop doesn't say much about the lathe any more; he reminds us of Dale Nish's article about it in *Fine Woodworking* a decade ago (Issue No. 41) or of an illustrated section of Nish's book *Master Woodturners* (Provo, UT: The Artisan Press, 1985).

'Junk'

To those who suggest that the drawings in those publications look too simple, Moulthrop responds by saying, *'The lathe shown is entirely made of 'junk'. There is a salvage yard near here in which one could find anything: You could build a*

2. Close-up of mounting the faceplate with lag screws and electric impact wrench

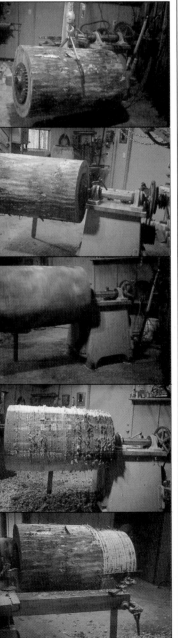

From top to bottom

3. Hoisting log up to lathe shaft. Note that faceplate is centred about the other end of log — the widest part of the bowl

4. The lathe shaft screwed into the faceplate — ready to roll! 1170mm 46" cantilever off the plate

5. 1300 lbs spinning for the first time and all smoothly. Of course only 50 rpm

6. First cuts to remove eccentricity — lathe performs admirably — no vibration! And the faceplate screws are proving adequate — thank goodness!

7. Cutting goes smoothly now. Rough shape beginning to form

DC-3 if you hunted long enough there for parts.' So lathe shaft, steel angles, belts, pulleys, bolts, motors, heavy tractor gears which he turns into faceplates, etc., are all made from 'found' material which many of the rest of us — particularly those who don't have his engineering/architect's background — just wouldn't recognize.

When I asked about mathematics required for designing the lathe, he suggested that a feeling for structural design was at least as important as mathematics (though I'd suggest this understanding must have a great deal of mathematics built into it). Moulthrop believes the junk yard is worth mentioning — even though he doesn't mention his by name — if only to keep would-be emulators wary of overpriced undersized woodworking-store items. The best craftspeople seem to know that a trip to the store isn't the

answer to every problem. We have to look within ourselves to figure out how to make do with the materials at hand or to improvise solutions.

The lathe shown here has five speeds. 50 rpm is the speed for turning the largest logs — like the one shown here. Other speeds are 60, 150, 200, 280. But this lathe is only used for roughing, heavy cutting indeed. From this lathe, work advances to a soak in PEG-1000 (polyethylene glycol), then to the finishing lathe, which has much higher speeds as required for trimming and sanding.

Some other issues struck this writer as being of interest to the citizen woodturner. I asked Moulthrop what he does with all the chips he creates. He 'shovels up' rather than sweeps the chips, but only when they get in the way. The chips are usually hauled off by his friends and neighbours who use them in gardens, garden paths, and the like. The roughing lathes work only green wood, so no dust is created. Do the byproducts of our woodwork meet similarly useful ends? Keeping the world 'green' has to be as important as keeping our shops clean. These techniques must work, for his shop always appears clean, and he certainly appears healthy!

Amateur turners often seem distressed at how rough their rough work looks. It's supposed to look that way. Isn't it wonderful that Moulthrop's photo No. 7 shows how rough

'rough shape' really means!

Photos Nos. 8, 9 and 10 show the rough hollowing process, but they belie the fact that the process can take days when the project is a very large vessel. We really can't expect instant gratification when we do a project — even some very simple projects take quite a bit of time. Working that time correctly, in an attitudinal sense, has to be part of the secret of any art or craft.

8. Exterior — all shapes cut and beginning to cut interior. Toolrest moved around to end

9. Close-up showing steps of cutting interior. 1830mm 6' lathe tool used here. See typical cuttings hanging from tool rest

10. Long reach for cuts down near the bottom. Tool extends over 915mm 36" from tool rest. This tool is 3355mm 11' long! — 63mm diam. at shank, left

11. All hollowed and time out for the kids to play

12. Backing off the faceplate. Hoist still needed as bowl still weighs 150 lbs or so

PEG

After rough turning, the bowl soaks about three months in PEG. When the bowl is taken from the tank, it is dried in a room where there's a dehumidifier running constantly; a bowl as big as the one in the photo may have to dry for up to three months. Then they are mounted on the finishing lathe where they are accurately trimmed down to finish thinness and sanded. The finish coats are then applied — usually four coats, sanding between each. Sanded (No. 400 or No. 600 grit) and polished with tripoli and rouge in oil.

Ninety days may be just the ticket for PEG-ing an item in Atlanta, GA. When I asked about PEG drying, trying to draw some comparisons to Wisconsin climate and small user purchases of the PEG

material, I learned that Moulthrop buys PEG in 55 gallon drums (each weighs 550 pounds). He adds 83

13. Off the lathe. Now removing the lag screws with the impact wrench. Wider shoulder at top will be removed on final turning. Now it soaks in a vat of PEG solution for 3 months

Ed Moulthrop beside the finished bowl

gallons of water to each (that's 1.5 units of water to 1 unit of PEG) for a specific gravity of 1.07. Moulthrop doesn't count January and February as soaking time (allowing the temperatures are too low then to get the penetration process underway), though I suspect we would-be turners in more northerly climes would have to move the operation indoors during more of the year than just January and February.

As the projects come out of the vats Moulthrop lets pieces drain off into the tank before moving them back into the shop to save wasting the PEG (which must be pretty costly,

then 10, then 5 per cent — now Moulthrop estimates his reject rate at around 1 per cent — that's only one failure per hundred! My failure rate is almost certain to remain far higher than this!

While the rough turning of a bowl the size of the one in these photos may take days, finish turning can easily be completed in a day — and with a lighter weight version of the same three tools. Abrasive materials are very important to the finishing schedule; Moulthrop starts with No. 36 abrasive paper, then 50, 80, 100, all the way to 600 on the finish coat.

Artists are apparently born, not made, but looking at Moulthrop's way of working may improve the ways we plan and execute our shop tasks.

We have to look within ourselves to figure out how to make do with the materials at hand or to improvise solutions.

even in the quantities in which he buys it). The PEG remaining in tank can be re-strengthened by adding more pure PEG until its specific gravity, as tested with a hydrometer, is 1.055 to 1.07.

Before remounting the PEG treated pieces on the lathe centres, they must be carefully measured to be as much on centre as possible — to get the minimum eccentricity at the most important part of the bowl. Again that sense of structural design comes into play.

Failure Rate

When I asked what percentage of such projects wind up in the fireplace because of curing failure, operator error, hidden defects, or the like, I was astounded by Moulthrop's answer. While learning, the number is big, perhaps 25 per cent. Then as you get experience, it goes down to 15,

Finishing

People who haven't found satisfactory finishes might be fascinated with the finish of Moulthrop's bowls. He begins by brushing on three or four coats of varnish, urethane or epoxy, sanding between each coat. Moulthrop didn't photograph these finishing steps *because there aren't many exciting sequences to show here as there are in roughing.* While it takes a lot of time — something many of us amateurs begrudge this most important part of a project — the finishing process really isn't spectacular, but if it isn't done thoroughly, the project won't last.

An important lesson to us is this last thought about finishing. The project has to last, or the poet who said '*A thing of beauty is a joy forever*' will have been a liar, and the artist's efforts will have been transitory rather than eternal.■

Born in 1963, Bob was brought up in Cranbrook, Kent, later moving to the small village of Coxheath, near Maidstone, where he now has his own studio/workshop.

Bob began turning just after the hurricane of October 1987. Self taught, he was soon exhibiting his work at local craft shows, mostly small items such as boxes, vases and simple bowls. As his experience grew so did his desire to make more decorative pieces.

Bob is probably best known to woodturners for his tools and accessories, but within the arts and crafts world is also regarded as a professional woodturner.

He now specialises in decorative bowls and hollow forms, gaining inspiration from ceramic and glass artists both past and present.

Bob's work has been bought by many collectors of designer crafts both in the UK and abroad. He has had a number of UK exhibitions and his work can be seen at most of the *Crafts Alive* shows organised by ICHF Ltd.

As well as being on the Register of the Worshipful Company of Turners, Bob has also been awarded Membership of the Society of Designer Craftsmen, and more recently accepted for the South East Arts Selective Index.

Photo 1 Tall designs with fairly straight sides are a good shape to begin with.

HOLLOWIN

BOB CHAPMAN

"How did you turn that?" is a question often asked of turners of hollow vessels. Here Bob gives some answers, using his own tools.

Questions I am regularly asked at craft shows and exhibitions are: "How do you hollow turn?", "Where do you start?" and "What tools do you use?"

With all hollow turnings there are a number of points to consider before starting out: the type of wood to use, the method of mounting the work on the lathe, the tools needed and, of course, the design of the piece.

The design is the first thing to deal with. The easiest shape for hollowing is one where the angle of descent from around the opening to the maximum diameter is fairly steep, such as a tall vase or a stretched spherical design (Photo 1).

A more squashed shape, or a design with a very shallow descent from the opening, will be far more difficult to hollow (Photo 2).

You also need to consider whether the design will retain a natural edge or be completely smooth and symmetrical. A natural-edged piece, especially if it has a bark inclusion or hole in the side, will be easier when trying to judge wall thickness and also help with the removal of shavings.

The latter option is safer when working close to the opening, but it can be more difficult to judge wall thickness, and if the opening is fairly small it can be more difficult when trying to remove the shavings.

Mounting the work is fairly simple, the method being largely governed by size, and whether it is to have a natural-edged opening or not. If a natural-edged piece, I prefer to use my own design of 1¼" Pinjaws (BCWA) (Photo 3).

Photo 3 The natural-edged blank is mounted on the pin jaws.

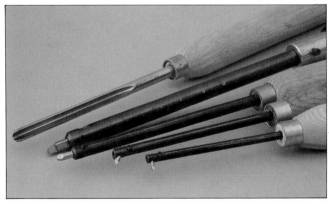

Photo 6 A bowl gouge ground for use in hollowing can still be used for conventional bowl work.

Photo 2 Squashed shapes with acute top angles provide a much greater challenge.

HINTS

Photo 4 The outside is rough turned — note the long handle for stability.

Using a spade drill, bore a hole about 25mm 1″ to 38mm 1½″ deep (depending on the size of the piece) in the top, then mount it on the chuck and you are ready to rough turn the outside and produce the main fixing (Photo 4).

Photo 5 Tall designs with vertical grain are rough turned between centres — note the large drive centre.

Before starting work on the piece, it's worth looking at the type of tools you will need to remove the inside. A number of different types are available for hollow turning, the ones you

If the piece is fairly tall and flat-topped, the work is normally roughed out between centres using a large 50mm 2″ two-prong drive (Photo 5). On larger, fatter pieces, it will be mounted on a screw chuck or faceplate to obtain the first fixing.

will need depending very much on the designs and size of the pieces you want to make.

On simple designs with fairly straight sides, an ordinary ½″ bowl gouge can be used to remove much of the waste, by grinding off one edge of the tool and using the lower edge in a scraping manner (Photo 6).

For large, fairly straight-forward pieces with an end grain structure, the DAHT tool by Rolly Munro can be used, but you will need quite a large opening to use it, and it's a bit pricey.

When working on fatter designs or pieces with a small opening, a few specialist tools are needed. For this example I shall be using my own design (BCWA) of hollow turning tools (Photo 7) which work in a similar way to those used by David Ellsworth.

Photo 7 A selection of tools used for hollowing out.

They have a cobalt/HSS cutting insert which can be set at 45 DEG to the main bar (80 DEG on the 5/16″ version) for getting under the top of the piece, and a second position in line with the bar for working the bottom area inside the piece.

There are also some miniature hollowing tools by Chris Stott

which may be used on small vessels up to about 75mm 3″ DIA.

It's advisable to fit fairly long handles to the tools used for the hollowing process, as this will help counteract the cutting forces on the ends. Many of my own tools have handles between 380mm 15″ and 760mm 30″ long, and are left unpolished to provide a better grip.

For this project I shall be using a piece of fairly straight-grained ash, which is reasonably free cutting and easy to work.

The piece will be of a stretched spherical design of about 125mm 5″ DIA, as this is a fairly easy shape to start with but still provides the opportunity of using angled-tipped tools to remove the wood from around the opening. Enough on groundwork, let's make a start.

With the piece mounted on the lathe, the first step is to rough turn the outside profile in the normal way and create the base to be used as the main fixing point for the remainder of the turning. For this piece I have turned a short spigot on the end to hold in the dovetailed jaws of a 4-jaw chuck (Photo 8).

▶

Photo 8 The blank is roughed out to shape — note the dovetail spigot for remounting.

On larger designs I prefer to use a small faceplate and glue block. First turn a flat-bottomed spigot on the base of the work about 63mm 2½″ DIA with a step of about 3mm ⅛″.

Then screw a piece of close-grained hardwood such as beech to the faceplate and turn a recess about 1/16″ deep to fit the spigot on the work (Photo 9).

Photo 9 The two mating parts of the glue block and faceplate ready to be joined.

If, when you glue the two together, you use a cyanoacrylate adhesive such as Hot Stuff, it will be ready to turn in just a couple of minutes.

With the work remounted in the chuck, the outside is finish-turned to the desired profile (Photo 10). It's a good idea to leave the base fairly stout at this stage to support the work during the hollowing process.

At this point it's often easier to sand most of the outside before any hollowing begins,

Photo 10 A ⅜″ bowl gouge finishes the outside profile with a shearing cut.

Photo 11 The 3″ Velcro sanding disc soon produces a smooth surface.

especially if the wall thickness is to be taken fairly thin (Photo 11). Otherwise problems can arise due to the work moving or not having enough rigidity to resist the pressures of heavy sanding if carried out later.

To begin the hollowing process, the first step is to bore a hole to the depth required using a drill bit slightly smaller than the desired finished size of the opening. For this I normally use a small spade drill held in an old drill chuck (Photo 12).

Here, I am using a ½″ spade drill, but I suggest you start by making a hole of about 32mm

Photo 12 A depth hole is made using a ½″ spade drill at low revs.

1¼″ DIA, until you gain experience. This will make it easier to hollow out, and also help remove shavings and gauge wall thickness.

With a little practice you should soon be able to reduce the hole size to around 12mm ½″ to 15mm ⅝″ DIA, depending on the size of the work.

The next stage is to remove as much wood as possible, using a straight tool. It's best to use the largest tool that will fit through the hole, first for speed of wood removal, and second for maximum rigidity.

I find the quickest method is to use the ¾″ hollowing tool with the insert in the straight position, although a bowl gouge ground as described before can also be used.

However, for this exercise, as the hole size is only 12mm ½″ DIA and will still be just under 15mm ⅝″ DIA when finished, I am using the ½″ hollowing tool (BCWA) with the insert in the straight position.

When using most hollow turning tools you will need to change your grip slightly from what you are used to. Tuck the handle along the underside of your arm and hold it close to your side (Photo 13).

You will notice the wrist is then almost above the tool when gripped by the right hand. The left hand controls the bar of the tool both in an overhand grip for roughing out and underhand with fingertip control for finishing cuts.

With the tool held in this position, you will find you can resist any downward pressure on the cutting tip much easier as your body and the tool become one.

I would strongly advise you to wear some form of face protection during hollowing, in case you cut through the side and try to deflect the debris with your face.

Begin hollowing by moving the tool in through the hole about 20mm ¾″ and bring the cutting edge into the side of the hole to obtain the cut, and then slide the tool down the side of the hole as far as possible. Repeat this process two or three times, removing the areas of wood in stages as shown (FIG 1).

During all the hollowing, check the wall thickness regularly. For this I use either my fingers, if the hole size allows, or double-ended callipers (Photo 14). It's wise to stop

Photo 13 The grip used when hollowing differs from that used on conventional tools — note the arm resting on top of the handle to resist any downward force on the cutting point.

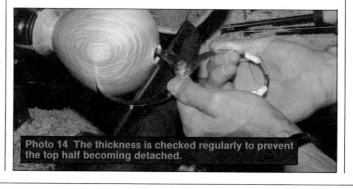

Photo 14 The thickness is checked regularly to prevent the top half becoming detached.

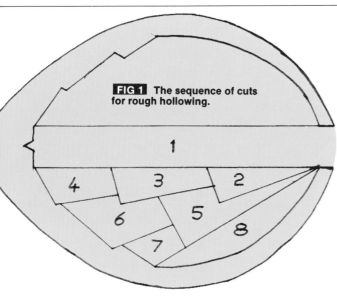

FIG 1 The sequence of cuts for rough hollowing.

rough hollowing about 25mm 1" from the bottom and leave the wall thickness about 12mm ½" thick at this stage, as you will need the support for finishing later.

Remove the shavings constantly. This can be done by using a small teaspoon, removing the piece from the lathe and shaking them out, or, if you have a compressor, by using an air gun to blow them out, but watch your eyes (Photo 15).

If shavings are not cleared regularly they can wrap around

the tool like spaghetti and cause the tool to spin.

After the bulk of the middle has been removed, the next step is to rough out under the top around the opening. For this operation I'm still using the ½" (BCWA) hollowing tool, but

Rippled oak and walnut vase 200mm 8" H x 180mm 7" DIA, x 3mm ⅛" T at rim and 6mm ¼" T at base.

Walnut burr vase made in two parts 280mm 11" x 180mm 7" DIA, 3mm ⅛" at rim and 8mm ⁵⁄₁₆" at base.

Photo 15 Using compressed air to force out the shavings is certainly the quickest method for small hole work.

Photo 16 Fine cuts with a ¼" spindle gouge refine the opening.

Coloured vessel in rippled maple, 150mm 6" DIA x 115mm 4½" H x 3mm ⅛" T.

Collection of hollow vases in rippled oak, tiger oak and walnut burr, largest piece 280mm 11" tall.

with the insert now at 45 DEG.

Starting at the opening, gradually bring the tool across until it starts to cut, then feed the tool in and around the inside profile until the wall is around 10mm ⅜" to 12mm ½" thick.

During this rough hollowing it's possible to take fairly large cuts, as there is little danger of going too far and cutting through the side. It's useful to file a series of lines on the top of the tool 25mm 1" apart, to give a rough guide as to where the tip is inside the work.

Before any further hollowing is carried out, you should refine the opening. I do this by using a ¼" spindle gouge to clean up the surface (Photo 16). I've left

this operation until now as I often use the edge of the hole as a lever during rough hollowing. The edge would be damaged if finished earlier.

Now you have roughed out the middle and finished the opening, you can begin to refine the inside down to the desired thickness. I suggest you aim for a wall thickness of no less than 6mm ¼" thick to start with, until you gain a little experience, as coming through the side of the work can be soul destroying.

To remove the last of the waste wood and refine the surface, I shall use both the ⅜" and ½" hollowing tools. On vessels with a fairly flat top angle, I would also use the ⁵⁄₁₆" hollowing tool.

First, using the ⅜" tool with the insert at 45 DEG, gradually bring the tip into contact with the wood just inside the opening until a small cut is gained.

▶

Photo 17 Finishing the inside with the ³⁄₈″ hollowing tool.

Slowly move the tool around the inside profile for a distance of about 38mm 1½″ from the opening (Photo 17).

At this stage it's normally easier to check the wall thickness using your fingers. Keep taking small cuts until the desired thickness is achieved over the area you are working on. Don't forget to keep clearing the shavings.

Repeat this process over the next 25mm 1″ or so using the ³⁄₈″ tool. I then change to the ½″ hollowing tool for the remainder of the hollowing.

Start with the insert at 45 DEG and carry on working in small stages at a time, checking the wall thickness constantly. You will need callipers at this stage.

Once you have reached a point inside, just beyond the maximum internal diameter, you can change the insert to the straight position (FIG 2). The

lower part is finished in a similar way to the top area by working in stages.

As you approach the base of the piece it's a good idea to increase the thickness slightly. This not only helps if you have trouble in gauging the thickness of the base correctly and so parting of the piece prematurely, but also gives the finished piece some stability when finished. It's helpful at this stage to use a depth gauge to check the thickness of the base (Photo 18).

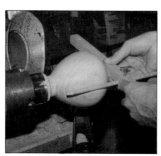

Photo 18 A simple depth gauge helps when working near the bottom of the piece.

With experience you will be able to take the walls much thinner and so gauge the thickness by listening to the sound of the wood being cut. This will then open up more areas of design where callipers cannot be used to check the thickness.

Once the inside is completed all that is needed is to finish the foot or base of the piece, carry out any final sanding required

Photo 19 A slow speed is used when cutting off — note the fine blade at the end of the tool.

and then treat the surface with the desired sealer or oil finish.

When cutting off the base select a low speed on the lathe. Using a narrow parting tool (here I am using the ³⁄₃₂″ fluted version), cut the base down to leave a spigot of about ½″ DIA. This can be taken further if the work is fairly light and balanced, although on natural-edged work I would suggest stopping sooner,

Photo 22 The base is sanded on a 2″ Velcro disc mounted on the lathe.

Photo 21 The small spigot of wood left is removed with a carving gouge. Watch your fingers.

as the work may break away with the force of the spinning piece (see Photo 19).

With the lathe stopped, cut through the remainder of the spigot using a small hacksaw blade, being careful not to mark the work (Photo 20). Next I use a ½″ spoon bent carving gouge to remove the remains of the spigot (Photo 21).

The base is then finished off on a 50mm 2″ Velcro sanding disc mounted on the lathe to complete the hollow vase (Photo 22). Now all you need to do is practice.

Photo 23 The finished piece in olive ash — 150mm 6″ x 125mm 5″ DIA taken to about 5mm ³⁄₁₆″ thick through a hole of 15mm ⁵⁄₈″.

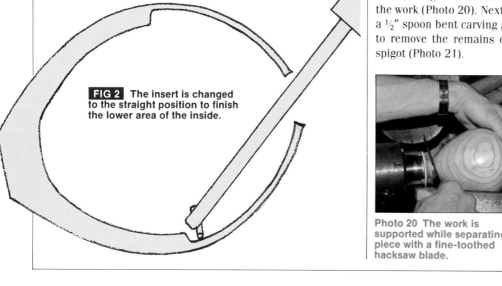

Photo 20 The work is supported while separating the piece with a fine-toothed hacksaw blade.

FIG 2 The insert is changed to the straight position to finish the lower area of the inside.

VAMPING A VASE

KEVIN HUTSON

Self-taught woodturner Kevin Hutson felt the need to branch out from conventional turning and create more artistically satisfying works. Here he adds a new slant to vase making.

Kevin Hutson, 35, has been woodturning for 17 years and is self-taught. He is now turning professionally.

Born in Brighton, Kevin served a three-year apprenticeship to become a carpenter/joiner, passing his City and Guilds to advanced level.

With 15 years practical experience behind him he then became a freelance draughtsman for an architectural design joinery manufacturer.

Having woodturned for commercial purposes in the past, he now enjoys creative turning.

His ideas come from observation of simple forms, such as the leaf of a plant or the exquisite lines of oriental architecture.

He is still using the Myford ML8 lathe he has used for the past 16 years. Earlier work was done on a modest drill attachment lathe.

To get the high standard of finish he now achieves has taken him two years of perseverance.

Kevin has been influenced by people like Ray Key and Vic Wood, whose work he much admires.

He is a member of the Guild of Sussex Craftsmen and is also listed on the Craft Council register.

After using wood for practical purposes as a carpenter/joiner for several years, Kevin has long felt the need for wood to be recognised and admired as a form of visual art.

He is married with two children.

Kevin Hutson, 20 Valley Dene, Newhaven, East Sussex.

After years of conventional turning and having reached a satisfactory finish to my work, I felt the need to be more creative. I began to concentrate more on design and aesthetics in my turning.

The idea for the following vase came from a piece of pottery I saw which inspired me to attempt it in wood.

The first stage in the making is to select your wood. I have chosen English ash, which has been through sawn. I use two methods of forming the vase, depending on availability of wood and grain.

In both methods, the grain is matched to the vase, as this is important to the overall effect. FIG 1 shows the first method, working on wood about 50mm 2" thick which you cut on a bandsaw to a 305mm 12" DIA.

Using a marking gauge set to half the thickness of the wood, mark around the circumference. Then cut the wood in half, following the gauged line with a handsaw.

FIG 2 shows the second ▶

FIG 1 **First method of matching grain to vase.**

305mm 12" DIA.

Marking gauge is set to half the thickness of the wood. Gauge line to be cut with handsaw.

Section through end grain.

50mm 2" thick.

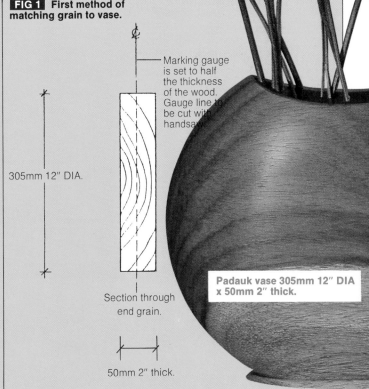

Padauk vase 305mm 12" DIA x 50mm 2" thick.

'I admire quality glassware and pottery designed with balance and proportion, and apply this to my turning.'

FIG 2 Second method of matching grain to vase.

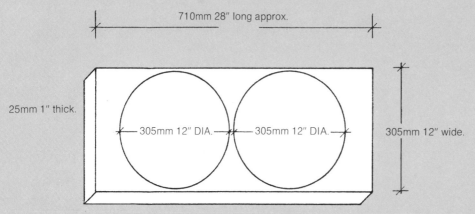

710mm 28″ long approx.

25mm 1″ thick.

305mm 12″ DIA. — 305mm 12″ DIA.

305mm 12″ wide.

Blanks to be cut on bandsaw. Mark out blanks close together to ensure match up of grain, but leave enough space between for bandsawing.

FIG 3 Method of matching the grain before turning.

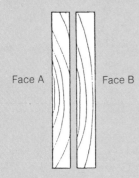

Face A   Face B

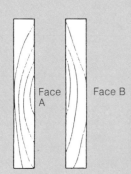

Face A   Face B

This is achieved by reversing Face A to become the inside of the vase, but Face B stays on the outside. This applies to both methods of forming the vase.

method of matching grain, with the selected wood measuring about 710mm 28″ long x 305mm 12″ wide x 25mm 1″ thick.

Mark out two circles as shown, with a compass, keeping them close together to ensure match of grain. But leave enough space between them for bandsawing.

FIG 3 applies to both methods. To get grain to line-up before turning on the lathe, face A is reversed to become the inside of the vase, but face B stays on the outside.

The two circles of wood are superglued and clamped to the centres of the two outside faces (Photo 1). I use superglue for

speed. Glue surfaces must be perfectly flat for good adhesion.

The circular blocks are used to avoid excessive wood wastage. The blocks are also used for reverse chucking purposes to form a spigot. I use a Multistar Duplex chuck with C jaws and a ring faceplate.

The two outside faces are turned (Photo 2), ensuring both profiles and diameters are equal. Having turned them, a permanent finish is not necessary at this stage.

Photo 2 The two outside faces are turned.

Photo 3 The bowls are reversed and the insides turned.

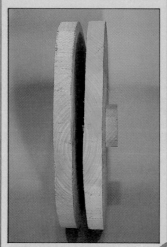

Photo 1 The two circles of wood are superglued and clamped to the centres of the two outside faces.

The bowls are now reversed (Photo 3) and the insides turned. The wall thickness needs to be exactly the same, the reason becoming apparent when the vase is eventually cut. I use a thickness of 4mm $\frac{5}{32}$″.

The rim (Photo 4) needs to be flat across the diameter for gluing. Check with a straight edge. The rim has to be about 6mm $\frac{1}{4}$″ wide.

Photo 4 Rim needs to be flat for gluing.

At this stage both inside surfaces can be brought to a finish and sealed (I use Danish oil), ensuring none of the sealant comes into contact with the rim, because of the glue reaction.

Before gluing, I clamp the two bowls together dry, to check for a good joint, to mark with a pencil where grain matches and to decide the pressure needed for clamping.

The two bowls can now be glued together (Photo 5). To clamp them, I use a pillar drill, which enables me to control the pressure with the depth gauge on the drill.

Photo 5 The two bowls can now be glued together.

Ensure all rim surfaces are covered, using a good quality PVA glue, and leave under pressure for eight hours.

When dry, the vase can be remounted on the lathe (Photo 6) for removal of one spigot with a bowl gouge and for sanding to the desired finish.

Photo 6 When dry, remount vase on lathe.

Photo 7 The remaining spigot is removed.

The remaining spigot now needs to be removed (Photo 7). To do this, I place a 355mm 14″ sanding disc onto the lathe and sand the spigot off. This will have to be hand finished to match the rest of the vase.

Onto the exciting stage for me, as the vase begins to take shape (Photo 8). Because I turn different size vases, there are no set measurements used. I simply try to achieve the balance and proportion I admire in quality glassware and pottery.

Photo 8 The vase begins to take shape.

To cut the base and neck of the vase, I first mark the base with a pencil and cut it on the bandsaw, using a sanding disc to get it perfectly flat.

I mark with a pencil freehand, bearing in mind the neck should be in proportion with the base. The neck is then cut on the bandsaw and smoothed off. I use a small drum sander attached to the lathe and then finish by hand.

The base stand is the last job to be done. For this, I use an off cut of the same species. The dimensions are shown in FIG 4. The overall design and measurements need to be 180mm 7″ long x 63mm 2½″ wide x 8mm ⁵⁄₁₆″ thick.

I get the shape simply by drawing freehand onto the off cut, then roughly cutting on the bandsaw before obtaining the correct shape more accurately with the disc sander.

All surfaces are then finished by hand to the same standard as the vase. ▶

FIG 4 Indicates design and measurements to the base stand.

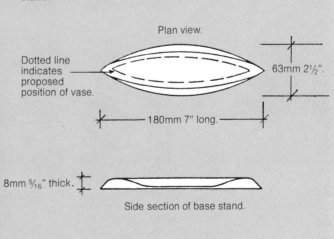

Plan view.

Dotted line indicates proposed position of vase.

63mm 2½″.

180mm 7″ long.

8mm ⁵⁄₁₆″ thick.

Side section of base stand.

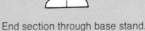

End section through base stand.

With all parts completed, the vase can be glued to the stand, clamping dry first of all to check for a good fit. A cork block is put between the neck and the drill chuck to avoid damaging the vase.

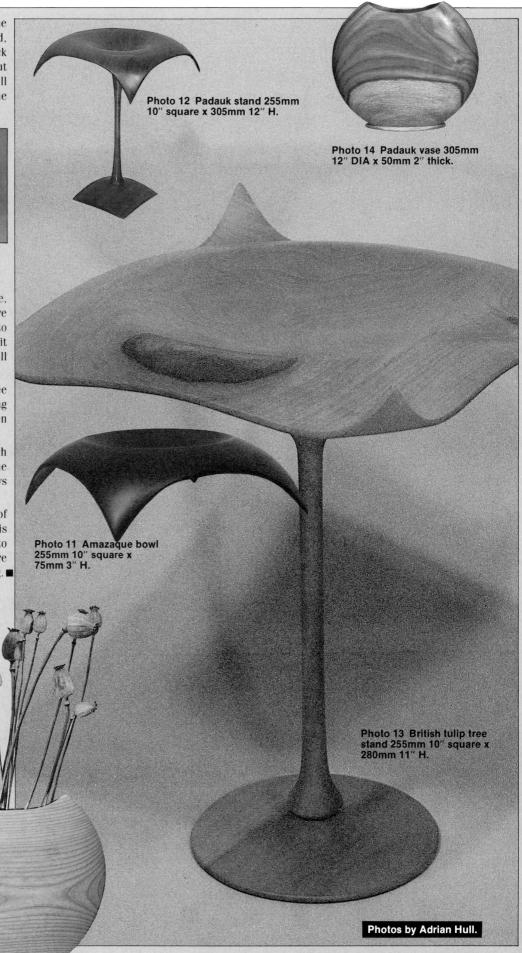

Photo 12 Padauk stand 255mm 10″ square x 305mm 12″ H.

Photo 14 Padauk vase 305mm 12″ DIA x 50mm 2″ thick.

Photo 9 The completed vase, English ash 305mm 12″ DIA x 50mm 2″ thick.

When applying the glue, ensure the vase is in the centre of the stand, before leaving it to dry for eight hours. Then take it from the clamp and remove all traces of glue.

For the finish I use three coats of Danish oil, leaving eight hours drying time between each coat (Photo 9).

I hope you have as much enjoyment as I do in making the vase, which Photo 10 shows displaying dried poppyheads.

Photos 11 to 15 show some of my other work. My ambition is to own my own gallery and to give tuition to those who share an interest in creative turning. ■

Photo 11 Amazaque bowl 255mm 10″ square x 75mm 3″ H.

Photo 13 British tulip tree stand 255mm 10″ square x 280mm 11″ H.

Photo 10 Displaying dried poppyheads.

Photos by Adrian Hull.

PHILIP MOULTHROP
LIKE FATHER, LIKE SON?
BOTH MORE AND LESS THAN YOU MIGHT BELIEVE

Hugh Foster was born in Kansas and raised in suburban Chicago. He received a BA from Carthage College in 1966 and has been teaching English at Lincoln High School, Manitowoc, Wisconsin, ever since.

Hugh has been a woodworking hobbyist since 1967 and a woodworking author since 1984. He has had some 200 articles, reviews, project plans, tool manuals and books published since he took up the pen. Currently available worldwide is his *Biscuit Joiner Handbook*, published by Sterling in the US and Cassell in the UK. He has become increasingly interested in turning and hopes to be a regular contributor to *Woodturning* for the foreseeable future.

HUGH FOSTER

Philip Moulthrop was born into more favourable artistic circumstances than most woodturners, for his father is Ed Moulthrop, the noted woodturner/artist. It was during his boyhood that the senior Moulthrop began developing the large tools and machines that have helped him create that body of work which is uniquely his own.

Just as Ed began as an architect and water colour painter before inventing a style of woodturning, Philip earned a BA in biology, then, after a stint in the navy, completed law school. He presently spends two days at the law and the remainder of the week turning. Philip's children show no interest in turning yet, but we can always hope. Having seen the work of the second generation, I'm hoping to see a third.

Through the years, Ed Moulthrop hasn't taken many students, but sons are a special case. From his father Philip has learned technique, tool design, and methods. Perhaps equally important, father is still there for discussion and idea sharing. Topics at these sessions include tools, lathes, etc, PEG, finishes, blacksmithing, and the like.

Ed Moulthrop says that Philip adds about 30 bowls to each of his shows. 'You'd expect the son of Antonio Stradivarius to make violins, not ukuleles. Someone *else* may take a different tack'. Fair enough.

Two postures while cutting the outside of the bowl with the lance

With an electric chain saw, Philip ensures that the bottom of his blank is both relatively smooth and quite square

Drilling to start the inside ↓

Spinning the blank on by hand

Note the use of safety equipment; these postures barely begin to indicate what a physical, almost athletic event one of Philip's turnings is. There is no wasted motion — and no wasted time. Watching Philip turn is closely akin to watching perfection

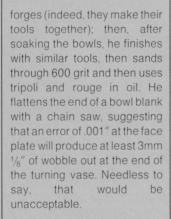

Turning the inside

Close-up of turning the inside

Then, when I asked whether he was a turner in father's mould or original or traditional or . . ., Philip said that he certainly learned his father's methods, but as he did, he began to make his own style, such as tall vases and raised elliptical bowls. Like every other good artist, he follows the tradition in his own way. While Philip's shop and even some of his turnings look similar, he is plainly working from a different 'vision'. Happier than most artistic families, they work 'together' without the clashes of artistic temperament that have become legendary in some other families.

In this article we'll explore some of the differences a generation can make.

Equipment

Philip's equipment is much like his father's. He uses the Nish/commercial (Moulthrop signature) tools on smallish bowls (suggesting they are best used on bowls of about 150-200mm 6-8") and heavier versions like those his father

forges (indeed, they make their tools together); then, after soaking the bowls, he finishes with similar tools, then sands through 600 grit and then uses tripoli and rouge in oil. He flattens the end of a bowl blank with a chain saw, suggesting that an error of .001" at the face plate will produce at least 3mm ⅛" of wobble out at the end of the turning vase. Needless to say, that would be unacceptable.

While the equipment is similar, there are some differences as well: His lathes are a bit heavier. While Ed's lathes are on a base of 20mm ¾" plywood on corner frames of 50-100mm 2 x 4s. Philip's lathe, 20mm ¾" plywood on 100mm x 100mm 4" x 4" legs. It doesn't take an engineer to see how much stronger this base will be, though an engineer might call this an exercise in overkill. Additionally, Philip added a motor lift to ease changing belts and an electrical outlet for accessory tools. He also uses an enclosed sanding room to confine dust. Ed loves Philip's

new shop with all improvements designed in. Like his father's shop, though, Philip's shop contains a chalk board for sketching — even at life size. This is surely one of the reasons his vases or bowls always appear to be 'in proportion'. He says the tall ones are at least 380-460mm 15-18" high, and if the proportions aren't right, they will be heavy and off-balance appearing. That, of course, would be unacceptable.

Safety

Philip uses more safety equipment than does Ed. *(My purpose in mentioning this is not to suggest Ed is not working safely. Indeed, on those occasions I've photographed Ed at work, I knew that the biggest safety risk in the shop was a fellow with a camera who was standing altogether too close, all the while offering altogether too much distraction.)* When asked to comment about his interest in safety, he observed, 'I am *very* careful using equipment such

as the band saw. I always wear safety glasses or face shield. After PEG soaking and subsequent drying, there can be lots of tension in the wood. Sometimes pieces explode as they crack, etc., on the high speed lathe. Caution is always the watch-word.' He comments thus about the gloves he wears while turning:

'I wear these gloves to protect my fingers and hands from being pinched between the tool and tool rest. They also protect my hands from being "burned" during sanding and help to hold the sand paper without being cut. They do not cause much slippage of the tools.'

Philip recalls an accident of his father's in which, while turning a large bowl, Ed was thrown across the shop when his large hook tool caught on a railroad spike buried deep in the tree, resulting in a broken tool and a few bruises. That accident, resulting from a freak encounter between man and nature, is more than bad enough.

Many of the bowls in the drying room have failed after the first ↑ step

But, more importantly, many ↓ more haven't

Bowls from the drying room ready for finish turning

Bowls which have been finish turned, awaiting finishing

Bowls with minor patches awaiting finishing

These small bowls are drying →

This larger bowl is drying while turning ever so slowly on a ↑ 'spare' lathe.

The final turning/sanding room is isolated from the other shops to help keep the mess to a ↓ minimum

Accidents caused by our own negligence are inexcusable.

Even though his work is more obviously safe looking, it also appears to go faster, as he pumps the handle of the tool *up and down* as well as *in* while cutting. The about 50-75mm 2-3″ of vertical hand motion gives the lance a paring motion as it contacts the wood. Monochrome photos 3-4 show the use of safety equipment as postures barely begin to indicate what a physical, almost athletic event one of Philip's turnings is. There is no wasted motion — and no wasted time. Watching Philip turn is closely akin to watching perfection.

Rhythm

Philip makes about 150-200 bowls a year; this is perhaps 25-30 per cent more than his father makes, but he quickly discounts the number, reminding us that his father's bowls are generally much larger than his. Depending on the size, Philip will do the same steps on 25-30 bowls at a time. He notes that the rhythm of the

shop is very important. If we get out of rhythm, there will be great lags of unproductive time between stages. There's little point in being unproductive. Every motion should count. Working on a fairly large batch of bowls helps keep things going smoothly.

He produces a variety of sizes. The largest vase was about 1015mm 40″ high, from pine. Ed observes that Philip's bowls are 'smaller than mine, but bigger than nearly all others', and 'His work is as good as mine, but slightly less expensive'. This probably means that Philip's bowls are good investments for the collectors who buy them, for their value is certain to rise.

Native Timbers

Like his father, Philip eschews tropical timbers for those native to his region, the south-eastern United States. When asked about his favourite material, Philip said, 'I like soft maple and magnolia for the smooth cut; box elder for its bright red colour; walnut and cherry for

rich grain. Each type of wood has its own special characteristics.' He went on to allow that cherry is probably his all-time favourite.

Philip uses a wide variety of woods — like father, very interested in unusual patterns and/or colours. While he doesn't 'believe in' staining wood, he will darken cherry by changing its pH with sodium hydroxide (lye). He has a few blanks of American chestnut, long believed to be extinct, left in his collection; the bowls he makes from these he will keep for himself. Most of his wood is obtained from tree cutters who have already cut the trees; sometimes, probably rarely, he and his father purchase logs from a commercial log/lumber yard. The photos of the work in Philip's in-shop gallery will indicate the variety of wood he works.

What's the fascination with turning? He says there is a constant fight with the ever-changing nature of wood, but he then goes on to say that the term is too negative, for this

'fight' is the key component in the project's intrigue.

PEG

No one else uses PEG as completely as do Philip and Ed Moulthrop. While there have been a couple of books written about it, they get vague very quickly about how this substance really works and how it changes the nature of the wood, especially regarding finishing. PEG can cause no end of problems, but Philip and his father are working out practical solutions to them. What do they know that's not in the text books? For example: Water based finishes, like Hydrocote, *(a finish so good that when I build a furniture project, I use several easy-to-apply coats of Hydrocote in preference to any other finish)* readily available in the United States, don't work with PEG. On a furniture project, this material dries water-white (absolutely clear), but on PEG it turns white. Epoxy finishes seem to work best on PEG treated wood.

For some, being the son of someone famous in the field would be a real hindrance. They might wonder whether they're successful because of or in spite of their fathers. Philip needn't worry about that. Besides exhibiting with his father at the Signature Shop,

The shapes of Philip Moulthrop's bowls are generally different from the shapes of his father's; note the bowl top right is made of American Chestnut, long believed to be extinct

'Watching Philip turn is closely akin to watching perfection.'

Atlanta; Gump's, San Francisco; Hand and Spirit, AZ; and Heller Gallery, NY; Philip's work may be seen at American Details, Inc., Coconut Grove, FL; Naples Art Gallery, Naples, FL; The Works Gallery, Philadelphia; The Elements Gallery, Greenwich, CT; Gallery Pro-Art, St. Louis, MO; Magic Mountain Gallery, Taos, NM; LaJolla Gallery Eight, LaJolla, CA; and Walter/White Fine Arts, Carmel, CA. Additionally, his work is in the permanent collection of at least seven museums, and has been in invitational exhibitions, and juried shows and competitions, a listing of which is upwards of three pages long.

Let's close with a bit of dialogue:

Foster: How do you call yourself: artist or woodturner or_____????

Moulthrop: Mostly a woodturner. It sounds less lofty.

Foster: Artist/craftsman?

Moulthrop: Craftsman.

I'm not sure you'll agree: Craft is but the beginning of art, and as the accompanying photos show, Philip Moulthrop's bowls and vases are indeed artistic. ∎

TRANSLUCENT NORFOLK ISLAND PINE BOWLS

Ron Kent lives in Honolulu, Hawaii. As if that were not enough, his translucent wood bowls are in private, corporate and institutional collections including Museum of Fine Art (Boston), Metropolitan, American Craft, Cooper-Hewett (New York), Renwick Gallery (DC) and the Vatican.
Ron is 59, married with two grown-up children. He is a graduate engineer (UCLA, 1957) and a 30-year veteran stockbroker. He resigned as vice president of a New York Stock Exchange firm to start a small independent brokerage office and a municipal bond mutual fund of which he is now president. Ron teaches adult education courses and hosts a weekly call-in radio talk-show on personal finance and investment. He also conducts a special 8-hour seminar for artists and craft people titled *Practical Finances for Impractical People* and seminar workshops on personal creativity. Ron spends about fifteen hours a week at his woodturning and sculpture. His bowls command premium prices among collectors and he readily admits that he likes being well paid for doing things he loves to do. 'It's as if I were a nymphomaniac working as a Park Avenue callgirl!'

RON KENT

Hawaiian turner Ron Kent is well known for his beautiful translucent bowls made from Norfolk Pine. In this article he throws light on the process he has developed to give them their unique lustre. The process takes up to six months and as many as 60 finishing cycles.

A few years ago (*quite* a few, come to think of it) my wife gave me a lathe for Christmas. She had seen it on sale at a neighbourhood store for 35 dollars, which included two blades for the built-in saber-saw attachment.

Though I'd never used (or wanted) a lathe of any sort, I did want to show my appreciation, so I went out on the beach to find some promising driftwood. I clamped the machine to my workbench, sharpened an old wood-chisel and

made something that looked akin to a clumsy wooden whiskey bottle. And I was hooked!

I gradually upgraded my equipment through a couple of commercial models to my present home-made minimonster and experimented with various tools. For materials I've always preferred local findings to the exotic imports. Collecting logs and cuttings has indeed become a hobby in itself.

Translucent Bowl
180mm 7″ high x 230mm 9″ diameter.

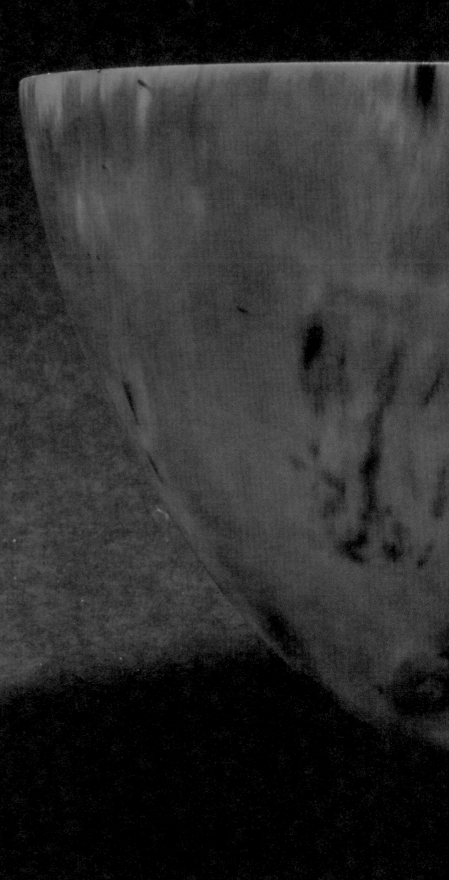

Technique has evolved with experience, but my primary challenge has always been to figure out my own way to do things, designed around my personal limitations on time, money, tools, materials, knowledge and skill.

During my first few years of woodturning I worked with every type of wood that grows in Hawaii, plus some strange unidentifiable varieties that have floated to our shores as driftwood. I've always viewed each log as a unique challenge of what most pleasing shape I might get from it, and what techniques to use to achieve that shape. (I am much more concerned with the finished product than I am with the methods and techniques of achieving it.)

My early experiences with Norfolk Island Pine were a natural outgrowth of my experiment with local woods. I don't remember where I found my first Norfolk Pine log, but I worked it as I would any new piece of wood.

The tree itself is characterised by symmetrical layers of branches sprouting uniformly around the circumference, at regular intervals. Each branch comprises a vermilion knot extending radially from bark to pith. There may be as many as eight such knots in each layer. I quickly recognised these knots as an important element of design and shaped the bowl around them.

The finished bowl had an attractive dusty-ivory colour with grey-black wash of spalting. As is my wont, I rubbed on a layer of boiled linseed oil and was amazed . . . for about two minutes . . . at the rich golden hues and sharp dark contrasts. Even as I watched, the oil soaked into the wood leaving a dull matt finish only slightly nicer than the original wood.

Simple enough! I oiled it again and immediately restored the lush surface . . . for another two minutes.

The oiled surface was too beautiful (and I too stubborn) to accept this kind of defeat. Somewhere there must be a point at which the wood would retain its lustre. Perhaps if I poured oil over the surface? Immersed the whole bowl in oil? Immersed it and allowed it to soak for hours, days, or weeks?

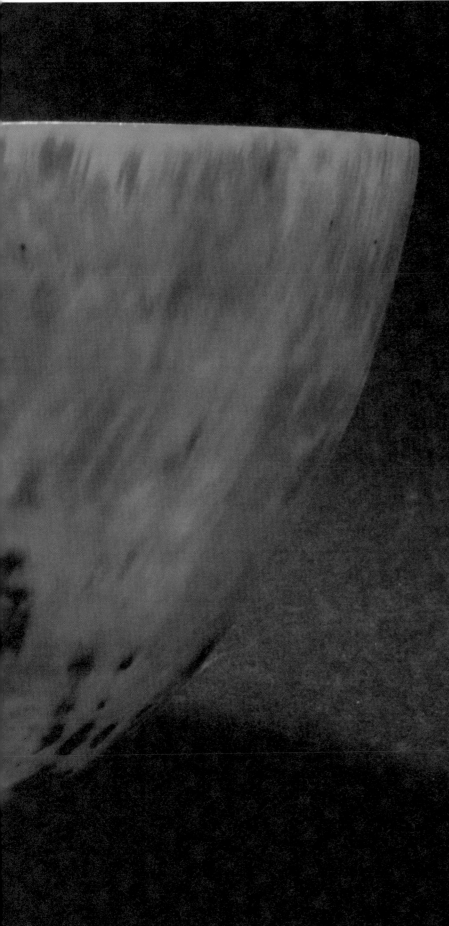

THE PROCESS

Here is the process that finally evolved. Before removing the bowl from the lathe, I sand it with 60 grit, then 80, and finally 100. This is the finest I use to this point.

I remove the bowl from the lathe, cut off the shafts and grind/sand the surfaces smooth. The entire operation takes about fifteen minutes and will be described in detail later.

The bowl is then immersed in a large vat (over 100 gallons) of boiled linseed oil and allowed to soak at least twelve hours. It is then removed, wiped dry, and allowed to stand at least one day. This soak/dry cycle is continued at least a dozen times over the next few weeks. Experiment has proved that duration of the soaking period is immaterial. Six months is no different than overnight. It doesn't matter how long it soaks, only how many separate times.

The next phase in my finishing process is also a cyclical one. Instead of soaking, I apply the oil with a pad of 150-grit wet-or-dry sandpaper, lightly sanding both surfaces of the bowl. Then I wipe dry and allow to stand at least overnight. This cycle may be repeated as many as fifty times over the next few months.

As the process nears completion, the bowl retains the translucent lustre longer and longer with diminishing patches of drying.

Occasionally I'll go to finer grades of sandpaper (320) for the last dozen treatments, but not usually. (Perhaps we'll discuss my ideas of design, aesthetics, and art-versus-craft later in this or a subsequent article.)

I consider the oiling process complete when the translucence and lustre remain undiminished. Then I repeat the cycle another half-dozen times.

Now comes two or three applications of carnuba paste wax applied with a pad of 0000 steelwool *and polished off with a fresh dry pad of the same!*

Translucent Bowl.
254mm 10" high x 305mm 12" diameter.

Translucent Shallow 'Bowl'.
102mm 4" high x 533mm 21"
diameter.

'Bottle-Form'.
203mm 8" high x 305mm 12"
diameter. (Not hollow)

Translucent Bowl
254mm 10" high x 355mm 14"
diameter.

Translucent Bowl
254mm 10" high x 305mm 12"
diameter.

THE PROCEDURE

Now let's go back and take a more detailed look at some of the steps I've been describing.

After stripping the bark off my log, I mount the log between centres. A typical log may be 510mm 20 inches in diameter by 460mm 18 inches long and weigh about 80 pounds soaking wet. Newly felled Norfolk Island Pine is indeed soaking wet to the core.

My lathe has a 50mm two-inch-diameter live spur centre and a heavy-duty ball bearing dead centre. I put my lathe in 'neutral' and jockey the log around until it is statically balanced. Hmm . .

Maybe a bit of clarification is in order.

First the bit about 'neutral'. I drive my lathe with a 220 volt, 1½ horsepower motor connected by fixed-ratio pulley to a junkyard *automobile transmission*. A second fixed-ratio pulley goes to the head-stock. Lathe speed is varied simply by shifting gears, and *neutral* allows free turning of the shaft.

In the best of all possible worlds we could determine the exact centre of gravity of each log and mount it to turn smoothly at the flip of our switch. With care and enough trial-and-error recentring you can approximate this condition if you are more patient and less willing to compromise than I am. Myself, I'll settle for an eyeball centring. By using a slow initial speed for my first rough cutting (250 rpm), even the heavy logs cause very little vibration.

My first cutting operation is to form a true cylinder, and the first tool I use is a broad heavy scraper.

I sharpen the tip and apply the tool in such a way as to *cut* in the same fashion a plane cuts a board. This operation produces a continuous, uniform 'chip' that gathers on my tool, up my arms and finally in a mountain at my feet as the log is virtually 'peeled' to a 50mm 2 inch diameter at the headstock end. This will be the bottom (outside) of the bowl.

The right hand (tailstock) is shaved to the largest diameter cylinder the log will allow and this full diameter carried back out about half the length of the bowl, then tapered to the 50mm 2 inch diameter spur centre.

It isn't all scaper work. I do alternate the cutting chore with a 25mm 1 inch roughing gouge.

The end which will be the top of the bowl is first trued with a half-inch round-nosed scraper and/or a 15mm ⅝ inch deep flute gouge. Now we're getting to the things I do differently.

Using the 'fingernail' configured gouge I start shaping the *inside* of the bowl. I cut a relatively small diameter hollow around a central shaft. *This shaft will protrude from the inside bottom of the bowl to the dead centre as long as my bowl is on the lathe!*

I cut in until I encounter the knots. Up to this point we've been talking about *craft*. Now it's time to become an artist. Everything I've described has been preparation and now it's time to start designing my bowl.

I study the configuration of the knots and try to determine the most aesthetically pleasing way to incorporate them into the design of a vessel. If I cut straight across them I will have a pattern of circles. A diagonal cut yields ellipsoids and a flat cut along the knot gives a starburst radiating from the pitch.

THE AESTHETICS

Artistic design deserves an article of its own. For now, suffice it to say that I apply my own aesthetic criteria and design my bowl's interior to highlight and interact with the knots, the pith and the grain characteristics of the log.

I design, cut, scrape and sandpaper the interior of the bowl to completion before I get back to the exterior. And I do it with the previously described shaft coming out from the centre of the bowl.

When the inside is completed, I start cutting the outside contour to match. I alternate between a variety of gouges for most of the external shaping but the final fine cutting is done with the tip of a spear-point 'scraping' tool.

The outside contour follows that of the inside (of course) with a thickness indicated by the size and shape of the vessel. My typical 510mm 20 inch bowl may be about 2.5mm 0.10 inches thick at the rim, gradually increasing to 6.25mm .25 inches near the bottom centre.

I tend to like a 'foot' that seems to levitate my bowl above a supporting surface, and a hollow coved effect within that foot. (Now we're back to design aesthetics.)

A quick series of sandings with 60 then 80 then 100 grit, and the bowl is ready to come off the lathe.

The inner shaft and outer nub are ground out using a rotary rasp and a die grinder, followed by flap-sanders in the same die grinder. I can't dawdle over this step because the wood is drying and shrinking even while I work on it. If I take too long I am likely to have one or more shrinkage cracks along the rim, so it is crucial to immerse the bowl in oil as quickly as practicable.

I've already described the immersion/dry and oil-sanding/dry cycles earlier in this article. I'd like to explain how and why the process works so well, with my wood. I'd like to, but I can't. There's an awful lot I myself don't understand about it. The process evolved as a combination of intuition, trial-and-error, and lucky accident. Indeed it still is evolving, because I certainly have not stopped experimenting.

Let me close this article with an invitation. Would you like more detail on any of the steps I've described? Clarification? Please write to this magazine and I'll answer for all of our readers.

And if you ever come through Hawaii, be sure to give me a call. ∎

Terry Martin was born in Melbourne in 1947. A graduate of University of South Australia, and University of New England, he has had a satisfying and adventurous life travelling the world in various capacities, including Stage Manager of the Royal Opera House, Covent Garden, Ski Patrol in Austria, geological exploration in the Pacific Islands and Migrant Education in Australia.

A growing appreciation of fine craft work was heightened by several years spent in Japan and when Terry returned to Australia he decided to pursue his interest in woodcraft.

Terry believes that woodturning allows use of limited timber resources for maximum effect. Much of the wood he uses is recycled, such as fence posts or railway sleepers. Influenced by Japanese ceramics and other crafts, he believes that the natural faults of the timber should be allowed to remain to enhance the work he does on the wood.

The Ball-and-Socket Chuck

TERRY MARTIN

'John's boxes are a great puzzle for turners and discerning buyers.'

A regular segment of the Woodturners Society of Queensland monthly meetings is 'show and tell' where members bring in their latest pieces for perusal, discussion and constructive criticism.

Different members are nominated each month to adjudicate discussion or give their opinions of the offerings. Recently I was one of the discussion leaders and, after a cursory glance at the table of

pieces, I started picking them up one by one to comment. I hadn't really taken notice of individual pieces and when I picked up a strangely lopsided lidded box I thought 'another remounted piece'. I took a breath to start commenting on how it had been done, but then couldn't continue. I couldn't, for the life of me, see how it actually had been remounted. There was a pregnant pause while a hall full of members waited for me to pronounce judgement. Then came a voice from the back of the hall — *'I'd better rescue you and explain how I did it!'*

John Rogers, draughtsman and sometime woodturner, was the culprit. John says that one of his greatest thrills in turning is to come up with something completely different. As most of us know, that is very difficult today with the sheer number of inventive turners at work all over the world. But I think John might have done it here. I was so impressed that I visited John's suburban Brisbane workshop to see him do another.

John likes working in mangrove, a wood that is available near Brisbane and which cuts easily. Perhaps more important to John is that it scrapes very nicely, as he likes to use this technique on his boxes. First John makes up a set of templates out of scrap cardboard. If the work is not absolutely spherical, with the inner and outer surfaces concentric, it is very difficult to get a result.

Departure

To start, John hollows the lid in the usual way (photo 1), checking that the hollow is perfectly spherical by regularly inserting

Photo 1

Photos: Terry Martin
Diagrams: John Rogers

Photo 2

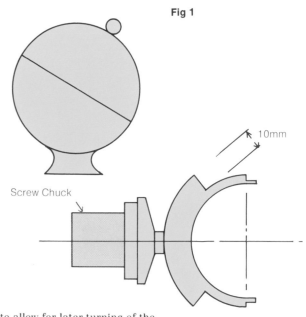

Fig 1

Screw Chuck

10mm

the template (photo 2). Then he cuts a lip on the base to accommodate the lid, jam-fits the lid on and brings the tailstock up to finish the outside (photo 3). A small knob com-

Photo 3

to allow for later turning of the foot (fig 1) and then parts off the base (photo 6).

Photo 6

Photo 4

Photo 5

pletes the lid (photo 4). John hollows the base, again using a template, and then shapes the outside. This is where the job starts to depart from usual practice. John only shapes the outer base about one-third of the way (photo 5). He leaves a step of about 10mm thickness

Photo 7

Fig 2

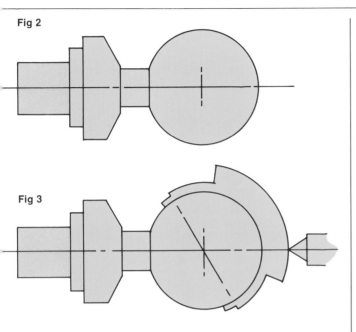

Fig 3

The next step involves turning a partial ball from some scrap timber (in this case pine) equal in diameter to the inside of the base (photo 7, fig 2). Now the need for accuracy becomes apparent. The base is ready to be chucked onto the ball (photo 8, fig 3) where it can be pivoted to give the required amount of 'tilt'. The tailstock is then brought up and the foot can be turned (photo 9). When it is the required shape, John removes the tailstock and finishes the underside of the foot. To prevent slippage, he tapes the base to the ball. When John's 'offset ball' was finished, he proudly exhibited the result (photo 10). The finished boxes are a great puzzle for turners and discerning buyers (photos 11 and 12).

Photos 10 and 11

John has been turning for four years and still manages to bring a fresh approach to his work with a bit of lateral thinking. He said that this idea came from a lot of doodling and thinking about ways of rotating work around the central axis. To show how unselfish John is, he said his hope was that 'somebody may now develop this technique a step further or think of an idea of their own to foster woodturning'. I don't know if it has been done before, but this ball-and-socket chuck fooled me and I really enjoyed learning how from the man who thought of it. ■

Photo 8   **Photo 9**

Photo 12

BELGIAN ROOTS

'I never force a piece of wood to be a salad bowl. It's a raw material, but living and talking.'

PAUL PEETERS

Woodturning in Belgium is not the open-hearted craft it is in the UK. Most craftsmen jealously guard their trade secrets in an almost medieval way, but here one of the country's few top professionals describes his work.

I was surprised to hear there are nearly 30,000 woodturners in England, including amateurs. In Belgium I know of only four or five professionals turning bowls and vessels, and five or six small workshops producing table feet, chairs and stair rods on copier and automatic lathes.

But, you have to know that Belgium is a tiny country, split into three regions, with three languages: French in the South, Dutch in the North, and German in the East.

The best known woodturners in Wallonie (the South of Belgium) are Peter Quist, Christian

Paul Peeters turning a bowl.

Ploumen, his wife Sabine, Jan Van Hoye and myself. But more about my work later.

The other four mainly turn salad bowls, using regional woods. In Belgium, we have a lot of fruit trees and forests with acacia, elm, cherry, ash and maple. We have park trees too, with yew, maple burl, goldrain (laburnum) etc.

I don't personally know any woodturners in Flanders (North Belgium), but I know there exists the De Draaiers Guild, a brotherhood of about 150 amateur woodturners.

Personal protectionism is a feature of Belgian craftsmen. By this I mean that everyone works in his own workshop and jealously guards his own working methods and know-how.

Woodturners are polite to one another, but that's as far as it goes. I asked one a technical question and was told: "All I do is secret."

Another, 72 years old, when asked by a fellow woodturner for permission to visit him at work, replied: "I have been turning for 50 years, and no-one has entered my workshop until now."

Exhibitions

I don't know how the connections between the English or the American turners are, but I observe you organise a lot of meetings and exhibitions together.

Woodturning magazine shows the need for contact between craftsmen. What are Belgian woodturners fearing?

If a craftsman has personality and skill he will do things his way, but some advice can just help ▶

The 'briar' root.

The 'waste' at the bottom of a
newly planted vineyard.

A heather bush.

Sifting through with a pick axe.

The loaded van, nearly ready to
return to Belgium.

you to get better, without becoming a copy-cat.

This excessive protectionism has many disadvantages. It has, for example, led to the woodturners' craft being largely unrecognised by Belgian people.

Their attention will be drawn to a sanded and polished turned piece, whether functional or not, but they won't understand why. Usually they say, "That's expensive," without appreciating why, and the work that went into it.

I am lucky because my shop is next to my workshop. So when a customer sees my work in the shop and is interested, the conversation often continues into the workshop, where I can demonstrate the stages between tree and finished piece.

Then they say: "It's not expensive. We didn't understand anything about your work."

The Belgians love wooden objects and decorations in the home. But only because it's wood, not because of the craftsmanship. As woodturning work is not well known by Belgians, they can't tell the difference between a good and a bad bowl.

They do not always appreciate that this bowl is too heavy, that the thickness is irregular, or that the form is badly balanced.

We have a long tradition in the use of ceramic objects, but wooden vessels, in the past, were reserved for animals, or the poor.

Old notions die hard, and today it's difficult to get people to accept nice, new forms of wooden objects and to teach them the difference between what is good and what is bad, and why.

'Asked by a fellow turner for permission to visit him at work the 72-year-old replied: "I have been turning for 50 years, and no-one has entered my workshop until now." '

Woodturning in Belgium has never been acknowledged as an art or, less pretentiously, as noble work. You will never see turned wood in an art gallery, alongside ceramics, pottery and other kinds of sculpture.

I deeply regret this, and don't exactly understand why we have this situation. The simplest explanation, but not I think a valid one, is that there are not many woodturners in Belgium.

Another, more important, reason is that woodturning is linked in people's minds with more general traditional woodworking, such as carpentry and joinery.

When a woodturner asks for permission to exhibit in an art gallery, the answer is always the same: "Woodturning? Sorry, but it's craftwork."

I remember an article in **Woodturning** (see page 28) where Philip Moulthrop was asked whether he was artist or craftsman. "Craftsman," he replied.

The difference between art and craft is a long-running debate, but in Belgium it's been decided: woodturning is craftwork and must therefore remain cheap.

Baffles people

Whenever I present a non-functional piece it baffles people. "What use is it for?" they ask.

I think pieces that require long research, whether technical or aesthetic, deserve better than craft fairs and markets.

I make two kinds of products. The first is well made functional pieces such as lamp feet, fruit, rattles, salad bowls etc., suitable for craft markets or craft shops. I often call them 'food works,' because they are wanted for use.

My second product is more special and I get a thrill from making it. Four years ago, I found heather burls (tree heather — Erica Arborea —or bruyere in France, the root of which is used for briar pipes) in the South of France.

It grows in the garrigue of the Hérault district, near Montpellier, Béziers, and is difficult to extract, as it grows between rocks.

I had to find an easier way to obtain the root burls. Now I'm looking in two places: where a new road is being dug in the mountains, and where wine growers are planting a new vineyard.

In the latter, all plants growing in the wild garrigue are bulldozed to the bottom of the field. I only have to be there at the right time to pick through the débris. It's a bit like potato picking.

I part-clean the burl roots on the spot and bring 1,000 kgs back to Belgium. All those plants are useless for the native people, but I love to make something from waste, to recover or recycle it.

Back in my workshop, I handle the root before turning, looking at it carefully to find the best

▶

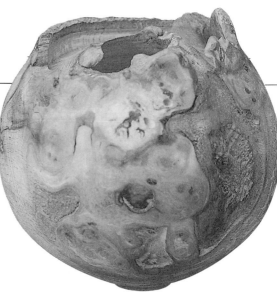

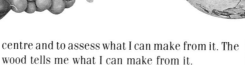

A selection of Paul Peeters' gallery works.

centre and to assess what I can make from it. The wood tells me what I can make from it.

I never force a piece of wood to be a salad bowl. It's not plastic. It's a raw material, but living and talking.

I won't cut a burl or knot for the sake of form. This must be determined by the structure of the wood. That's why I hardly ever buy wood. I prefer to find interesting pieces in nature, at the mercy of walks and chance.

Woodcutters and garden contractors know me well and supply what I am searching for, which is simply everything that doesn't interest the other woodworkers.

In my locality, I sometimes find birch and beech burls in the forests, abandoned by woodcutters because they can't split them. Of all the wood they cut, only these bits interest me.

Before turning a heather root, I brush the root with a wire brush to clean out stones and earth. Sometimes I find stones embedded within the wood, causing tools to break when they meet them.

If the stones are interesting and well-placed I let them stay, turning the wood around them and taking care not to touch.

I often stop the lathe during turning to look at the surface of the piece, once the form is defined, to make the nicest parts appear. I leave some parts unturned.

The burls are like planets, you can see continents, mountains and craters. The weight of a piece accentuates this idea of a planet.

The fact that I don't always empty a bowl or hollow a vessel is not a sign of inability. I do turn hollow vases, balls and dishes more decorative than useful.

To finish, I sand pieces with 180 grit paper. Next I put Sumatra oil on them. After two days, when the oil is dry, I polish the turned surface (only the parts which have been cut) with a pad soaked in shellac and alcohol. I think it's the best finish you can find.

I like to play around with the polished and crude parts, the rough and the smooth, of my 'planets' and vases. You don't only look at these pieces, you need to touch, to fondle them too.

Some of my finished pieces can be seen on these pages. I show these works principally in my shop and at craft meetings in Brussels and Germany. My best customers are Germans, Americans, Japanese, employees of the European Commission — and sometimes even Belgians! ■

Forager's feast

by Alec Jardine

To take wood no-one wants and turn it into something useful or beautiful is one of the joys of woodturning, as a South African turner discovered when he 'foraged' wood from a pile of off-cuts.

A few weeks ago our youngest son came home for the weekend. His first words of greeting were, "Where did you scrounge those bits of wood which are lying in front of the garage?".

At first I was a little put out at the implication that I was a scrounger. But on second thoughts I realised he was right. I had scrounged that timber.

I'd taken four railway sleepers to our local sawmill to have them cut into planks while I waited. The job was to take about an hour, so I walked round the mill to kill time.

Off-cuts

As usual, I made my way to the huge pile of off-cuts to see if there was anything usable. There were two pieces I

▶

Photo 9 Three of the finished bowls.

*Photo 1
The 'scrounged' wood.*

wanted, but when I pointed them out to the sawmill owner, he laughed.

"That big piece there is just a rotten offcut from an old plane (platanus acerifolia) brought in by a customer last week", he said. "When we started sawing we found it was so soft with decay that we decided to leave it here.

"My men have been using it for firewood, but it doesn't even burn well, they say. Take it by all means. It's of no use to me."

Kiaat

The smaller offcut was a piece of kiaat (pterocarpus angolensis) and, knowing my interest in woodturning, the sawmill owner added: "That will make quite a nice bowl".

So yes, I did 'scrounge' the two pieces (Photo 1), though I prefer to use the dictionary definition of 'forage'. I suppose it's a natural reaction of most woodturners when they see a bit of wood no-one wants, to take it and try to make something from it.

Whatever the case, the immediate effect of my son's remark was to make me examine the two pieces more closely, and that weekend I bandsawed them to give me the most usable sizes for turning bowls.

I started with the kiaat, for it was of a more manageable size, squaring it off on the bandsaw and then marking out as big a bowl as I could. This was roughly 300mm 11 ¾" (Photo 2).

The piece had quite a bit of sapwood, so I turned the bowl from the heartwood side, so the lighter colour of the sapwood would form the larger portion of the base.

This decided, I now cut the bowl blank from my piece of 'foraged' kiaat, attached this securely to a 75mm 3" faceplate and mounted this, in turn, onto the lathe.

Kiaat is an Afrikaans word for teak, which to some extent the wood resembles. It grows, as its Latin name implies, extensively in Angola, but is also found in central Africa and the northern parts of South Africa.

Kiaat can grow up to 20 metres high and is considered one of the most useful trees in these regions, used in a variety of ways, from boat building to making food bowls, for it shrinks and distorts very little from green to dry state.

The reddish brown heartwood works well, takes a good polish and is thus a highly favoured furniture wood. It's colour and peppery, spicy smell reminded me of iroko, another central African wood.

The kiaat cut cleanly and smoothly, and apart from a tendency for heat to build up in the chisel's cutting edge, the rough shaping of the shallow bowl's outer wall was soon and easily accomplished.

Sunflower

I next brushed sunflower seed oil onto the newly cut surface, sharpened up a square ended scraper, and carefully cut the outer wall to a smooth finish.

The contrast between sap and heartwood looked promising. I next cut a recess for the expanding 60mm 2 1/8" expanding collet that I used in my precision chuck and tested for fit.

The base was then sanded using 100, 220 and 360 grit. The combination of sunflower seed oil and fine grit papers gives a very pleasing end result.

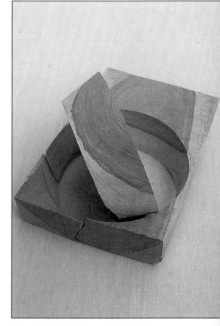

Photo 2 The kiaat blank.

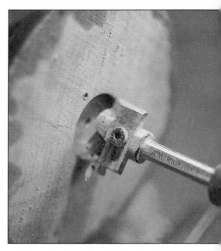

Photo 3 Using the Ridgway expanding bit to establish a large, deep hole.

Photo 4 The finished kiaat bowl and the waste from which it was cut.

Photo 5 The 'rotten' spalted plane blank sawn from waste wood.

Photo 6 The partly turned plane blank, showing the brown rot.

Photo 7 The blank now doctored with epoxy and sawdust mix

I'd recently bought a heavy-duty Ridgway power expansive bit and was anxious to try it out, once I'd reversed the bowl into the expanding collet chuck (Photo 3).

Removing the inside of a bowl is my chief concern once I've reached this stage, and having a Forstner type bit which would remove large chunks with least effort appealed to me.

So, after securing the bowl in the chuck and checking it was centred, I adjusted the Ridgway bit to 50mm 2", cranked the lathe's speed down to its lowest level, and proceeded to drill the pilot depth hole into the top of the bowl blank.

The drill sliced into the wood, producing long ribbons of red-brown shavings. I had soon cut deep enough for the pilot hole and it was good to see how easily the bit had coped with the rather hard kiaat.

Gouge

I re-sharpened the 10mm ⅜" HSS bowl gouge I'd used for cutting into the bowl blank, boosted the lathe speed a little, and had soon hollowed out the bowl.

Again, I brushed the surface with sunflower seed oil, and then trimmed up the inside with a heavy bowl scraper. A similar succession of sanding grits, a coat or two of beeswax, and the bowl was complete (Photo 4).

A rather successful exercise in turning a 'scrounged' or 'foraged' piece of wood into something useful, even if I do say so myself.

The spalted plane

I soon realised as I cut into the spalted plane that it was indeed a fairly rotten piece of wood. I've long been

▶

The author

Alec Jardine lived in Kloof, Natal, South Africa, and was a professor at the nearby University of Durban Westville, until he retired at the end of 1992 and moved to Port Elizabeth.
Eight years ago his doctor advised him to take up woodturning to take his mind off the stresses of a busy academic life.
He bought an old woodturning lathe and has been hooked ever since.
He has learned most of what he knows about woodturning from books, magazines, videos and "all manner of mishap, short of the disastrous."
Richard Raffan's earlier books and video helped channel his interest towards bowl turning, and he now spends most of his spare time turning out a variety of bowls.
He enjoys the challenge of turning some of the more difficult Southern African woods, but rates plane and silky oak high on his list of favourite timbers.
Alec is fascinated by the unusual, and enjoys working with spalted wood, burls and parasitised woody growths. He has made a special study of spalting and has written extensively on the subject of fungal infection in timber.
He is married, and he and his wife have a grown-up family, who all support his hobby.

interested in spalted timbers, and now prefer to cultivate my own, so this piece was not what I would have called ideal.

Like the curate's egg, it was good in parts. But once cut, showed such spectacular spalt figure, that I persisted in my efforts and managed to cut out three respectably sized and fairly sound bowl blanks (Photo 5).

There was evidence of insect colonisation, as well, and I found the pinhole sized channels of Ambrosia beetles throughout the sounder portions of the wood.

I decided there and then to turn rather thicker walled bowls than I usually do, for the wood was dry and cracked, and even on the bowl blanks I had cut from the sounder section, spots of brown rot could be seen (Photo 6).

When I rough-turned the outside of the first blank, these sections of brown rot promised to pose a problem, for there were three areas where the wood was so crumbly that even with my newly ground chisel, pieces broke out and spoilt the wall's appearance.

Some form of repair was called for, and I decided to mix a two-part epoxy glue with sawdust collected at the base of the bandsaw into a stiff paste, and force this into the bad spots.

Soaking

First though, I thought it might be a good idea to strengthen the decayed fibres with a soaking of PVA wood glue, mixed with an equal part of water so that it would soak into these sections and supply some much-needed tensile strength.

So I turned the three bowls to the same stage and 'painted' in the diluted wood glue wherever I found 'punky' spots. The bowls were left to harden overnight, and I was pleased the next day to find the decayed sections had absorbed the glue tund that the brittle portions had taken on a rigidity previously lacking.

I now prepared the epoxy and sawdust filler and, with a pen-knife, forced

Photo 8 The larger spalted plane bowl

it into cracks and holes where the decayed wood had broken out, gradually building it up until it was just proud of the surface. Again, this was left to dry overnight (Photo 7).

The next evening, I finished turning two of the bowls and, although the wood was not as sound as I would have liked, managed to complete them.

I first turned the outer wall, later sanding this to a level I was happy with, then cut the cavity for the expanding collet and reversed the bowl into it.

Again, I used the Ridgway bit to drill a pilot depth hole, drilling it out cleanly with minimum fuss. Admittedly the spalted plane was a lot easier to drill than the kiaat had been, but the bit still proved a boon.

The subsequent hollowing of the bowl was a bit tricky, because of the varying degrees of wood softness in the wall, but it was done, and the final cuts with the heavy bowl scraper finished off that part of the task.

As is my practice now, with all timbers except green wood, I did the final smoothing cuts and sandpapering after generously coating the surfaces with sunflower seed oil.

Being as dry as it was, and with t┤ usual body having been removed ┤ fungal action, the wood greedi┤ absorbed the oil.

This, in itself, lent a certain body ┤ the wood which it had previous┤ lacked, and made the final turnin┤ easier than it had been when tackle┤ in its dry state.

Walls

As I said earlier, I had to turn t┤ walls thicker than I usually like to, b┤ the effect is still rather pleasing to t┤ eye (Photo 8).

Although the 'scrounged' timber┤ had not been of the best quality,┤ had nevertheless been able to tu┤ four bowls from it, three of whic┤ are, perhaps, only decorative. B┤ the kiaat bowl has already been use┤ for salad and has stood up well ┤ use (Photo 9).

The other three will be taken alon┤ when next we have a table at a craft ma┤ ket, and I hope they will prove the eff┤ has been worthwhile.

Now I have used up my 'scrounge┤ pieces, it's time to visit my friend┤ sawmill owner again, to 'forage' f┤ some more 'useless' pieces on h┤ waste pile.

Martin Nolte was born in Cologne, Germany, in 1960. His love for woodworking began with carving his own tobacco pipes from briar blanks in 1980, long before he knew what a lathe is for! After university studies in German, English and Journalism, he worked as a sub-editor for a daily newspaper in Bonn until 1986. 'To be an editor means you spend your day mostly at the computer and on the telephone', Martin says, 'and very soon I had the desire to do something completely different, more practical'. With the chance in mind to take over a relative's farm, Martin apprenticed on different farms and spent two years at an agricultural college.

Planning to build a spinning wheel for his wife, he discovered woodturning which soon became an obsession but has always remained a hobby. Now it strikes him that 'somehow woodturning has brought me back to journalism': An article he wrote about a woodturning course with Ray Key was so successful that he began to specialize in writing and translating articles about turning.

Currently Martin co-edits the German professional turners' journal, *Holz und Elfenbein*, and is just taking his first steps in organic farming. 'Both organic farming and creative woodturning are movements that have become important in the Eighties', he points out, 'and what's most important to me in both fields are the people I meet'.

HANS JOACHIM WEISSFLOG

A PROFILE BY MARTIN NOLTE

If 'artistic woodturning' is a synonym for 'turned bowls' in Britain and Ireland as well as in America and down under, it simply means 'turned boxes' in Germany. In a country with more than a thousand full-time production turners and only a handful of woodturning artists, attitude of the latter seems to be that wood is precious and small is beautiful.

A good example of this German attitude is the work of Hans Joachim Weissflog, a designer and turner from Hildesheim, a town near Hannover, Lower Saxony, Germany. 'Klein und fein' (German for 'small and fine') is actually his motto! Hans Joachim Weissflog's boxes can be seen at the International Frankfurt Fair and the New York Gift Fair every year. Two of his boxes have been selected for the 1991/92 exhibition International Lathe-Turned Objects ('Challenge IV'), currently being held at Northern Arizona University until the end of December.

Most of the following article has been translated from German by Helga Winter, a woodturner in Port Townsend, Washington, USA. I could not have written this profile without her help. We sometimes need to help each other across the Atlantic!

Genuine Boxwood is one of the heaviest European woods with a specific gravity of 93 ('0.93' in some countries). Because of its fine and dense structure, and its tendency to take an excellent polish, it has always been a preferred turners' material in Continental Europe. European Box is used for mallets, chess figures, printing cylinders, yarn coils, instrument parts, and last but not least, for all kinds of miniatures. In Germany, the yellowish wood is also used for industrial and mechanical purposes, such as rulers and slide gauges, because of its dimensional stability.

Many people know box only as a shrub, and even in the warm climate of southern France the maximum height of the box tree (*buxus. sempervirens*) is 6 to 8 metres (20 to 25 feet). Nobody would think of using boxwood as the material for large bowls! But for a turner like Hans Joachim Weissflog it is the ideal wood, since he is great in the small! The turned pieces of the

Ball-Box, Turned Broken Through. European boxwood and African blackwood. 50mm 2″ (open)

African Blackwood Box with loose rings in lid (lid turned from one piece of blackwood). 50mm 2" in diameter

Photographs by Hans J. Weissflog

To examine the wall thickness, Hans Joachim Weissflog likes to cut through a finished box from time to time

Ebony Box (with a touch of sapwood). 40mm 1⅝" x 60mm 2⅜" x 72mm 2¾"

37 year-old German turner, are not only true treasure pieces but also show a wonderful technical precision. It may not be easy to believe Weissflog's claim to have made 'the smallest box in the world' but if you see it you will: It has an outer diameter of 0.7mm (0.028″) and a wall thickness of 0.1mm (0.004″)!

It is easy to guess that boxes comprise the largest part of Weissflog's work, since no other turning project requires more precision and accuracy. How could a person, with a background like Weissflog's, work with anything else but precision?

Born in 1954 in Hoennersum, Northern Germany, Hans Joachim Weissflog began his professional career apprenticing as a mechanic at the age of 15. He worked briefly in this field and then studied mechanical engineering at the Technical School in Hildesheim near Hannover from 1974 until 1976.

Blossom Box. European boxwood root burr (open)

ENGINEER

'How does a mechanical engineer become a woodturner?' I asked Hans when I met him in his Hildesheim workshop to do an interview for this article. The turner's answer is short and to the point: 'because of my studies in design'. The unemployed mechanical engineer decided in 1978 to enrol in the four-year industrial design

diploma course at the Hildesheim/Holzminden College, 'because only a few students were enrolled in this field'.

The engineer, who until then in his own admission was hardly able to discern one wood species from another, discovered woodturning there, while studying industrial design in

Ball-Box Sculpture. Brazilian purpleheart ball box fitted into rough-edge piece of German bog oak

Professor Gottfried Boeckelmann's class. He was so taken by it, that he paralleled his studies in design with an apprenticeship as a woodturner with Boeckelmann, who is not only a Professor of Design but also a Master Turner. Boeckelmann's educational influence on German woodturners is probably without comparison in any other country.

It is obvious that Weissflog not only has perfected the technical aspect of turning during his studies, but also the aspect of design. A well-made box requires more than a tight fitting lid. If proportions are not balanced, a box appears ugly, regardless of its size. The proportions in Hans Joachim Weissflog's work are perfect. He prefers simple forms that come alive through clear lines, and he dispenses with decorations, except that he occasionally decorates his ball boxes with delicate inlaid rings.

On the other hand it is apparent that the designer always challenges himself technically. The

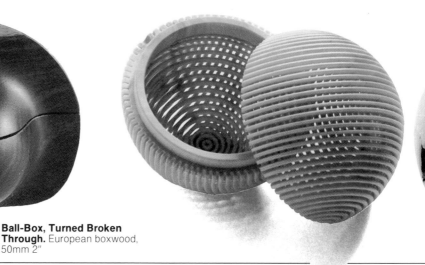

Ball-Box, Turned Broken Through. European boxwood, 50mm 2"

Saturn Box
closed

broken through ball box, first turned from boxwood only, is an example of that. The box has the appearance of a very fragile, airy construction

Saturn Box with loose natural-edge ring. European boxwood root burr, diameter of box 50mm 2″

Box with Lid Turned Broken Through. (Turned with two different centres.) Zapatero wood ('Maracaibo boxwood'), diam 62mm 2⅜″

high failure rate, even for an experienced turner with a strong technical background like Weissflog.

In 1991, the artist even increased the difficulty by making the same ball boxes from two contrasting kinds of wood — Genuine Box and African Blackwood (traded as *Grenadill* in Germany).

composed of tiny woodstrips, rather than something turned from a single piece of wood. The 'secret' is that each hemisphere was turned on the inside and outside with a shift in the axis of 90°, crosswise so to speak. The degree of difficulty involved in this work is illustrated by the

Brazilian Purpleheart Box,
closed

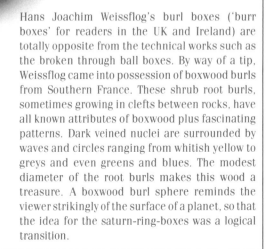

Brazilian Purpleheart Box.
40mm 1⅝″ x 60mm 2⅜″ x 72mm 2¾″

Ball-Box Within Ball-Box. Inner box like No. 1, 50mm 2″; outer box burr oak, 80mm 3⅛″

Hans Joachim Weissflog's burl boxes ('burr boxes' for readers in the UK and Ireland) are totally opposite from the technical works such as the broken through ball boxes. By way of a tip, Weissflog came into possession of boxwood burls from Southern France. These shrub root burls, sometimes growing in clefts between rocks, have all known attributes of boxwood plus fascinating patterns. Dark veined nuclei are surrounded by waves and circles ranging from whitish yellow to greys and even greens and blues. The modest diameter of the root burls makes this wood a treasure. A boxwood burl sphere reminds the viewer strikingly of the surface of a planet, so that the idea for the saturn-ring-boxes was a logical transition.

Box With Loose Ring. European boxwood root burr

ORGANIC

The pieces turned from boxwood burls have an organic appearance 'as if grown', despite the technical knowledge that was exercised in producing them. Some of the work is reminiscent of natural forms such as mushrooms, blossoms or funnels. Because the turner incorporated the outer rim of the burl, and did not destroy the evidence of the natural growth, this 'organic' appearance is strengthened.

This was not Weissflog's original intention. While working the burls he turned them down until he discovered healthy wood. This clear material provided the stock for the actual box. A disc from a cross section of the burl becomes the lid or the separately inlaid ring of the saturn-box. To advance in this manner does the preciousness of this material justice, the wood practically asking to be utilized to its utmost capacity.

Box. Madrona and ebony

Saturn Box and **Fungus Box.** European boxwood root burr

Hamburg, and the Corning Museum in New York — is created in a modest workshop. If you suspect that the learned mechanical engineer is turning his work with expensive equipment, you will be disappointed! Many a hobby turner has a more expensive lathe and a larger amount of machines. Everything that Hans Joachim Weissflog needs for his boxes he manufactures himself — be it the wooden chucks or the miniature turning tools for small parting cuts, fabricated from old key files.

Beautiful turnings, therefore, are not a question of large scale engineering, but a question of skill. For works like Hans Joachim Weissflog's, however, even skill is not enough. At work here is a true artist. ∎

Square Box. Burr padauk (Amboina) and ebony

'For two years I sold these natural-edge pieces like crazy', says the artist, 'however, suddenly the market for them seemed to be dead'. Weissflog, who sells a major part of his work at the semi-annual Frankfurt International Fair, has a simple explanation for the short-lived boom: 'Natural edge pieces from burls, in my opinion, are a trend'. Because of this, the designer focuses this year again on his original theme, the ball box —however, with new variations. The more complex works show the strong geometrical broken-through spheres, in contrast to the irregularly grown burls. The double sphere box (80mm or 3³/₃₂" in diameter) with an outer hull composed of two oak burl hemispheres is a good example.

MODEST EQUIPMENT

Weissflog's successful work — bought, among others, by the Museum for Arts and Crafts in

'Everything that Hans Joachim Weissflog needs for his boxes he manufactures himself. Many a hobby turner has a more expensive lathe and a larger amount of machines.'

Ball Box With Inlaid Rings African blackwood

Three Boxes with inlaid rings. Different woods

KURT JOHANSSON
THE MAN • HIS TOOLS • HIS WORK

JOHN HAYWOOD

Five years, ago, Tra Klubb, the magazine published by Luna, the Swedish tool company, highlighted the work of Kurt Johansson and the following year I was indeed privileged to handle some of the pieces shown in the article. These were most pleasing, all impeccably turned in native timbers and, apart from the quality of craftsmanship, I discovered that Kurt was a master of ring and hook tool turning. Finally we met at the Craft Supplies Buxton Seminar and he was persuaded to share his expertise with us.

Born above the Arctic Circle in 1940 in the little Swedish Lappland town of Moskosel, Kurt was an apprentice cabinetmaker for four years, then journeyman cabinetmaker. He further extended his skills by studying blacksmithing, toolmaking and others aspects of engineering, culminating in his training as a teacher. Since 1964 he has taught Swedish Slojd, for fortunately Sweden still ensures that craft skills are included in the school curriculum, unlike the UK and sadly North America is following this pattern too.

Kurt divides his time between teaching, turning for galleries and commissioned pieces, preparing for exhibitions and understandably he is in great demand in Sweden and elsewhere as a demonstrator. He enjoys experimenting with new tools and turning equipment and is a consultant to Swedish lathe and tool manufacturers.

Those who have met Kurt Johansson readily admire his masterly technique and both the modest and amusing way in which he imparts these skills. I watched several of his demonstrations and was most impressed by the way he quickly had a fellow turner performing so easily with the ring tool — a method previously so elusive! As a friend remarked, 'the best demonstration was by Kurt Johansson, he is a "natural teacher"'. That surely sums up the man.

Apart from his own experimentation with form and design, Kurt maintains the best in traditional Swedish turning. When he occasionally decorates pieces, these follow restrained regional patterns from the area where Johansson was born. This part of Lappland is the most rewarding for those visiting Sweden who wish to see the best of Same — Lappish crafts. Both men and women proudly maintain these delicate, refined and intricate crafts for which they are so noted.

Johansson now lives at Marieholm in Southern Sweden and the photo on this page shows him treadling away on his lookalike Chester Knight design. Basic drawings for this lathe appeared in an early issue of Fine Woodworking but Kurt's version is somewhat simplified and in the process looks more pleasing — an innate Swedish ability.

Kurt Johansson is working on a further illustrated article on the hook tool, so we can look forward to further enlightenment.

Kurt Johansson on his treadle lathe (a modified Chester Knight from 1975)

KURT JOHANSSON THE MAN

KURT JOHANSSON HIS TOOLS

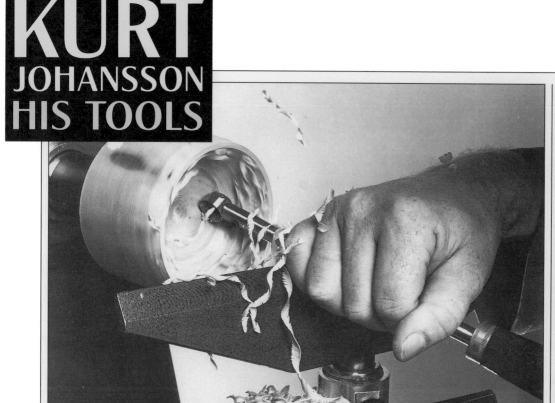

THE RING - TOOL

KURT JOHANSSON, SWEDEN

Photos 1-32 from top to bottom in three columns from left to right

The ring-tool is a very old invention. It has been in use in Scandinavia for hundreds of years, not as a tool for woodturning but for hollowing out wooden vessels by hand, especially by the Lappish people. Examples of vessels hollowed out by hand, for example wooden KÅSOR, can be seen in the Pinto Collection at Birmingham.

(KÅSA (plural KÅSOR) are traditional two handled Scandinavian drinking vessels. The bowl itself is round, widening upwards and ending in two handles. The latter are often elaborately carved, representing two animal heads, stylised forms or birds' heads and tails. — Ed.)

My first experience with the ring-tool was also hand-hollowing but soon the idea emerged that maybe the ring-tool could be used for woodturning. This was around 1968.

After some experimenting I found that the ring-tool was very good as a woodturning tool, the only drawback was that sometimes the long shavings got stuck in the ring. The remedy was to cut away about one quarter of the ring, that of course turned the ring-tool into a hook-tool.

Hook-tools are among the oldest woodturning tools but have changed little over the centuries and were almost forgotten until a recent revival.

Unfortunately the hook-tool is rather difficult to make in an economical way, that is why we now are back to the ring-tool!

The ring-tool closely resembles any other round bar turning tool, except that the end of the bar is drilled lengthwise to accept the ring assembly, the latter being secured by a tapped hole in the rod with an Allen screw. The cutter itself is about 25mm in diameter, attached to a 20mm long 6mm rod, which is then inserted in the end of the handled tool. The ring has two ground bevels, one outer and one inner. The tool works just like a deep fluted bowl gouge ground square across but is much faster cutting due to the thin cutting edge.

If you present a gouge wrongly to the wood you will have a dig-in. The same thing happens with the ring-tool except that it will be less severe, for the ring-tool is cutting at about the same height as the tool-rest and will be forced downwards and out of the wood.

With the ring-tool you can also adjust the ring in relation to the handle in order to avoid awkward working positions, such as leaning far over the bedways of the lathe.

Photos 1-4 show some of the different positions to which the ring can be set. Photo 5 shows a ring cut open.

When the ring is set as in No. 4, the tool will cut when pulled towards the turner. This is very helpful when turning undercut vessels in cross-grain.

ENDGRAIN

When hollowing out in endgrain, you have to start the hollowing from the centre of the workpiece and cut up to the rim. This means cutting with the grain. If you wish, you can drill out the centre of the workpiece using a 20-30mm Forstner bit.

With the ring mounted as in Fig. 1, the tool is very easy to control. But remember that the tool has to be held in such a way that the cutting edge is never horizontal. It has to be nearly vertical, or '5 past 7' as seen from the handle. Remember to keep the bevel rubbing all the time.

Photos 6-10 shows hollowing with the ring set as in Photo 1.

Hollowing with the ring set as in Photo 2. The lathe speed is approximately 1000 rpm.

Normally, only the side of the ring with the outside bevel is used, except when a very deep and narrow vessel is turned the side with the inside bevel is employed for cleaning up the inside bottom of the vessel. The ring is set as Photo 1.

If you are making a bigger vessel and want to cut faster, the ring should then be mounted as Photo 2. Beware! The tool cuts extremely fast and smooth. It is very easy to cut away much more wood than intended and you might ruin the work-piece.

No. 16 shows the finished result straight off the tool and the next photo shows the result after one coat of boiled linseed oil, with no sanding whatsoever!

When hollowing in crossgrain the ring is mounted as in Photo 3. The tool now works like a gouge, the cutting edge is at 90° to the handle just like a bowl-gouge.

Before hollowing with the ring-tool it is advisable to mark the thickness of the rim by making a groove with a small gouge or with a chisel.

Salad bowl, birch, chip-carved, diam. 250mm

The cutting is done from the rim and down to the centre of the bowl in order to cut with the grain. The ring-tool is held like a gouge pointing slightly upwards but, as the cutter is mounted under the handle and cutting at about toolrest height, the risk of dig-ins is minimal.

Due to the thin and very sharp edge, the ring-tool cuts very smoothly and easily through the wood, producing less vibration and ribbing.

As mentioned before, shavings sometimes get stuck within the ring especially when turning crossgrain. Photos 21-28 show turning with a ring cut open. No. 29 shows the finished bowl before sanding and the last shot, how the bowl was attached to the lathe.

SHARPENING

Sharpening the ring-tool is a very simple job. Just turn a stick with one end a tight fit in the ring, in conjunction with the stop-block (Photos 31-32). Adjust the latter to obtain the correct bevel on the ring, start the grinder and rotate the stick. Be careful not to grind too much or the ring will have a short life. The inside bevel is ground with a conical grindstone.

For honing I use a round stone of 12mm diameter 100mm long for the inside of the ring and a flat stone 12mm x 25mm x 100mm for the outside. Both are fine grit oilstones.

If you feel like trying the ring-tool, I suggest you try it on a softer wood like lime, to gain confidence before tackling harder woods.

Ring tools are manufactured by C. I. Fall of Sweden. Their representative in the UK is: Barry F. Cooper, CNS Marketing, Bon Sol Farm, Brightstone, Isle of Wight, PO30 4AZ. Tel: 01983 740744. Similar tools are produced by Robert Sorby Ltd, Athol Road, Woodseats, Sheffield S8 0PA. Tel: 0114 2554231.

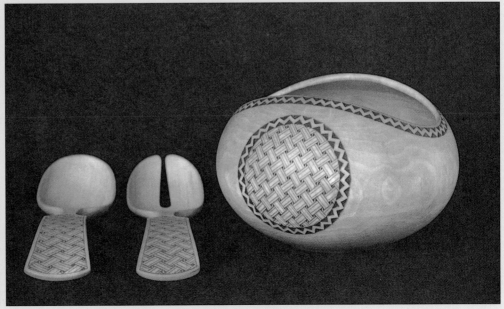

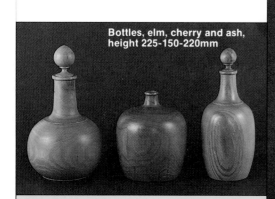

Bottles, elm, cherry and ash, height 225-150-220mm

KURT
JOHANSSON
HIS WORK

Jar, spalted birch, height 300mm

Goblet, spalted birch, height 200mm

Bowl with handle, alder, chip-carved, diam. 200mm

Jar, spalted alder, height 625mm

SHAPING THE LIP OF A BOWL

Tom Darby worked in education for many years before being appointed, in 1975, an Inspector of Schools in industrial arts. But the lure of the lathe was strong. He retired in 1987 to launch his own business – Baringa Woodcrafts – which he runs with his wife Margaret, in Wamberal, NSW.

Tom is currently writing a book for GMC Publications featuring 12 of Australia's finest woodworkers, each of whom will be contributing a unique step-by-step project. The book is due to be published towards the end of next year.*

* The book, *Making Fine Furniture*, was published in 1992.

**Vaughn Richmond
Sandalwood, vase with twig and leather, 120mm 4¾" x 100mm 4"**

TOM DARBY

Tom Darby looks at the work of two Australian turners and concludes that 'it's the shape that ultimately determines whether we become craftsmen or shaving producers and timber merchants'.

Last week I walked through our local shopping mall and before I entered the open display space at its centre I could smell the Camphor laurel and hear the whirr of a bowl being turned. The Central Coast Woodturners were showing their wares and some of their skills.

It's remarkable how many people find woodturning fascinating as it was difficult to see over the crowd standing three deep around the lathe. After I had watched for a time and inspected the display, I found myself listening to the comments of the prospective buyers. They were talking more about the gloss finish on the timber than the timber itself or the shape of the bowls. I wandered off thinking why I look for different things in turned bowls than most of those people I had observed. It doesn't mean that what I look for should be what others value; it's different and founded on a different experience of woodturning. I hope they were happy with their purchases and treasure them.

I don't buy many wooden bowls as I much prefer ceramic bowls platters and plates, largely because they are more practical for my lifestyle. I enjoy eating off wooden plates when I visit Robert Parker. They are hand carved, light, well worn and different but they don't go well in the dishwasher and there's nothing like eating off a white or pastel surface of a ceramic plate to enhance the colour of food. The wooden bowls I own are large, made from highly figured timber and are oil finished. They are both decorative and utilitarian and I enjoy feeling their shape. For me a bowl has to want to be touched.

Reflecting on the bowls in last week's display there wasn't one that I found appealing — that compelled me to pick it up and feel the movement of the curves on its surface, or turn it to watch the effect of the light in grain or the transition from concave to convex curve. Many of the bowls made by Richard Raffan or Vic Wood compel me to do that. There are an increasing number of woodturners in Australia who are joining these two master craftsmen in producing sympathetic shapes. What are the other variables in a bowl that give it appeal?

FINELY SHAPED

There are many variations on a theme in woodturning for there is a limit to what you can do with a block of wood. One of the principal aims for anyone working in wood is to enjoy it, but perhaps that enjoyment can be enhanced by working at something which is finely shaped. It's the shape that ultimately determines whether we become craftsmen or shaving producers and timber merchants. Perhaps it's important for all woodturners to critically analyse their success in forming an appealing shape as well as deriving satisfaction from producing something round.

Robinia bowl, 150mm 6″ x
120mm 4¾″ x 70mm 2¾″

Jacaranda bowl,
220mm 8¾″ x 100mm 4″ and
2mm ¹⁄₁₆″ thick

York Gum Burl, bowl, leather
and twig, 250mm 9¾″ x
80mm 3⅛″

VAUGHN RICHMOND

Recently I visited the Fine Woodcraft Gallery in Pemberton, Western Australia and saw on display for the first time some of Vaughn Richmond's work. The shapes are refined, walls fine and the lips of the bowls often brilliant. Vaughn's bowls, platters and vases have a sculptured detail on their outer edges. To shape an edge with a chisel, file and abrasive paper isn't difficult. To make the profile of those outer edges interesting and sympathetic with the form of the remainder requires a sculptor's eye.

Vaughn Richmond is self-taught and started turning as recently as 1985. Already he is established as an innovative turner whose work is enhanced with sculpture, texture and materials such as leather, precious metal and gemstones. He uses West Australian timbers extensively which he collects himself from forests in the south west and the dry interior. His work is sought for exhibition throughout Australia and is in private collections in Hong Kong and in the National Library in Peking. He was recently invited to exhibit at the World Economic Forum in Davos, Switzerland. The variety of shapes and lip treatments in his work have guaranteed a ready market for his work and he is currently preparing for a one man show at the Freemantle Arts Centre.

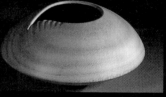

Swamp Banksia, platter with
twig and leather, 380mm 15″ x
100mm 4″

Swamp Banksia, bowl hollow
turned, 280mm 11″ x
120mm 4¾″

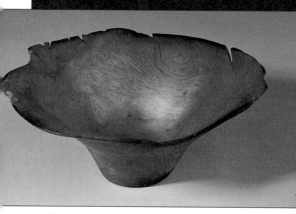

Sheoak burl, found on the
forest floor, 180mm 7″ x
70mm 2¾″

Jacaranda bowl,
140mm 5½″ x 110mm 4¼″ and
1.5mm ¹⁄₁₆″ thick

Australian Red Cedar, carved
bowl, purchased by
Powerhouse Museum, Sydney

Australian Red Cedar, detail
carved bowl

Australian Red Cedar, carved
bowl, 340mm 13⅜" x 150mm 6"

Australian Red Cedar, bowl,
Henry Kendall Collection,
Forestry Commission of NSW

GRANT VAUGHAN

Bowls don't have to be thin walled to be successful. But to leave the lip on a bowl full without making it appear heavy and uninteresting is an art. Grant Vaughan's bowls are both turned and carved and are an example of the sculptor's art rather than that of the woodturner. In some the bulk of the waste is removed by turning, the shape being generated with carving tools; in others there are recognisable faces which have been generated by lathe tools. Again Grant's success is in developing sympathetic shapes and it doesn't matter from which angle they are viewed, they are so well formed that the profile and shape is balanced. To produce those fine curved edges formed by intersecting curved surfaces requires a steady hand and great patience. They flow around the edge each terminating at a point where it immediately sweeps back to define a different shape as do the edge of leaves and flowers on many tropical plants.

Much of the timber used by Grant Vaughan comes from the forests of the north coast of New South Wales, near his home in Rock Valley out of Lismore. His work is in many private collections and Public Galleries throughout Australia. He also designs and makes furniture which features the same flowing curved lines. ■

Camphor Laurel, bowl,
300mm 12" diam.

A MEETING OF

REG SHERWIN

Our UK Contributing Editor profiles the work of innovative artistic woodturners Mike Scott and Hayley Smith.

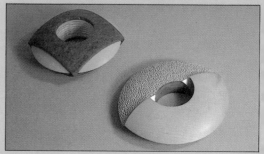

Above, **Bangles (left) sycamore and burr elm with silver wire inlay, and sycamore inscribed and gilded.**

Mike Scott and Hayley Smith live in a little cottage on Anglesey, North Wales. They met in Cheshire, where Mike was running his woodturning business from a craft centre.

A late college entrant, Hayley took an interest in turning during a three-year degree course. Early on in the course she discovered the college woodturning lathe and its few tools.

There was no-one on the teaching staff who could help her to develop the technical side of her interest, so she was advised to look for help outside college. Among the contacts she made was 'Chai', which is Mike's trading name.

After a number of visits Hayley had equipped herself with a chuck and a great deal more lathe experience than anyone on the college teaching staff, and she set about developing her skills.

Starting by designing and making wooden bangles from offcuts of wet timber which were too

Above,
Items by both Mike Scott and Hayley Smith show their differing styles.

Right, **Yew with carved bog oak inserts and silver wire inlay.**

small for Mike to make use of, she experimented with texture, colour, shape and finishing.

Initially her work was very similar in appearance to Mike's, primarily because she was using the same basic material, but she is now developing other themes. Having one of these pieces selected for the '91 Loughborough 40 was a great boost for her.

It is this work with blow torch, Dremel engraver and silver wire that she is best known for at the moment. She strives for perfection in finish before the work comes off the lathe, preferring not to hide poor tool technique under non-lathe produced embellishments.

MINDS

While she is looking to develop more ideas she still makes her 'bread and butter' bangles, and the care which she takes over each individual piece means that it can legitimately demand a realistic price.

Hayley uses a sketch book a great deal in her exploration into design. Quick though the lathe is, a sketch book is quicker, and what's more, the idea is recorded for ever and can be worked on and developed over and over again.

It's hard to believe now that artist Mike had a career in accounting in the early 1960s both in Britain and Australia where he lived from 1965 to 1976.

In the early 1980s he decided on a change of direction which led him to a one-year degree course in creative arts at Crewe and Alsager College. During this course he first came into contact with a woodturning lathe.

Towards the end of 1984 he set up a workshop with support from the Enterprise Allowance Scheme, and over the following year developed his lathe work. He held his first one-man exhibition in August 1986 and has since shown at numerous exhibitions and galleries.

He says: "In the process of seeking identity in my work I have studied and seen ideas and inspiration in vessels and other forms from many cultures. traditions and disciplines.

"With these influences in mind, I then strive for authenticity and spontaneity in my work, responding to prevailing moods, feelings and circumstances, while trying to express myself in an innovative way.

"Sometimes I follow through specific themes, other times I get excited by a new idea and go off at a tangent to try something quite different. I enjoy the infinite challenges and risks that are part of the process. Wood is alive, it moves, shrinks, puckers and splits presenting me constantly with new possibilities to deal with.

"The starting point for each piece I make is usually a rough-hewn chunk of wood from my wood pile which consists mostly of elm and oak burrs. Once I have chainsawed the piece into a roughly circular shape I attach a faceplate and mount it on the lathe.

"At this stage I have little idea what will evolve. As I start to remove wood in the turning process various possibilities emerge and the characteristics of each piece of wood (colour, hardness, age, grain, texture, moisture content) are a major influence in the development.

"I may exploit the texture by wirebrushing, ▶

Above, **Beech bowl inscribed and scorched, 100mm 4″ x 330mm 13″ DIA.**

Photo by Michel Focard.

... vessel, ...ed, ...nsawn, ...ed and ...dblasted ...chaeological ...es 1992) ...mm 15″

...tos by ...ley Smith.

Hayley Smith sanding one of her turned bangles

Mike Scott working on the square of beech blocks in his workshop.

Mike and Hayley discuss the possibilities of the square of beech blocks.   Photos by Reg Sherwin.

'The first time I saw Mike's work a few years ago I found it too different to be acceptable to my woodturner's eye, but I have come to accept most of it now, and to actually enjoy much of it.'

Bangles (clockwise from top)
yew incised; oak turned wet
and microwaved, elm scorcher
and wirebrushed.

Elm platter with silver wire
inlay, inscribed and scorched,
25mm 1" x 405mm 16" DIA.
This was selected as one of the
1991 Loughborough 40.
Photo by
Michel Focard.

Mike using the lathe-mounted chainsaw on a
large turned piece.

Elm vessel, turned, chainsawn,
ebonised and coloured
(Ancient Relic Series 1992)
610mm 24" DIA.

Oak winged vessel, turned,
chainsawn, carved and
sandblasted, 660mm 26" long.

Oak vessel, turned, chainsawn
and carved, 635mm 25" H x
305mm 12" square.
Photos by Hayley Smith.

leaving tool marks or ridges or by cutting grooves and segments with the lathe-mounted chainsaw. Colour may be affected by burning, scorching, bleaching, staining, painting or fuming in ammonia. Some areas may be sanded smooth to highlight an area of outstanding grain colour or pattern.

"Sometimes I use rope to encircle the exterior or make handles; iron plates, wire and nails for securing broken or cracked edges, or lacing with leather, catgut or cord over a split or fissure in the wood. I often leave areas from the outside of the tree surface to create sculptural effects.

"Recurring themes in my work have references to archaeology, amphitheatres, ruins and ancient relics etc."

Mike is a turner who qualifies the title by describing himself as a maker of wooden vessels. The first time I saw his work a few years ago I found it too different to be acceptable to my woodturner's eye, but I have come to accept most

of it now, and to actually enjoy much of it.

I particularly like his amphitheatre series, where the lathe-mounted chainsaw really comes into its own.

The couple work in separate rooms in the same workshop at the rear of the cottage, doing their own highly individual thing, but also on call to offer an opinion, advice or a helping hand to each other.

It was interesting to witness their exchange of ideas on the project which Mike was working on during my visit — a large block, made up of 50mm 2" squares of beech, glued together. Probably destined to be a reversible table top, but with the wall hanging option a fairly strong contender, it was part turned to see how the laminations behaved, then left to 'season in the mind' as it were. And their two highly individual minds are working on it.

As can be seen from the photographs, Mike's style of work is quite individual and it has established him in the eyes of UK woodturners as the leader in his field. Hayley is quickly gaining a name for herself in those same eyes as a young lady to watch.

Despite the obvious difference in their individual styles they work well together and while they have each had a number of both individual and group exhibitions, it surely can't be too long before they hold their inaugural combined show.

Mike Scott and Hayley Smith, Tan yr Efail, Llanddeusant, Holyhead, Anglesey, Gwynedd, North Wales LL65 4AD. Tel: 0407 730680. ■

'Mike's style of work is quite individual and it has established him in the eyes of UK woodturners as the leader in his field.'

WOOD-TURNED VESSELS OF GEORGE RADESCHI

LINDA BALIN

George Radeschi was born in Brooklyn, New York in 1945. Raised in Brooklyn, George attended public high school where he first became interested in woodworking. During college and afterwards, George became engrossed with the history and art of ancient cultures, especially those of native Americans.

With a strong mechanical background, George taught auto mechanics in high school while making fine wood furniture, decorative pieces and woodturned bowls and vases as an avocation. He now concentrates on intricately designed solid segmented turnings. Since 1987 the works have appeared in museum, gallery and corporate exhibitions. George's mechanical aptitude has enabled him to design and build woodworking machinery, unavailable on the market, to meet his specific needs.

He resides in Doylestown, Pennsylvania, with his wife Loretta, and son David.

'One day, while I was at an art exhibition about native American pottery, I looked at a clay vessel and wondered if it could be done in wood.' *George Radeschi*

Rosebud 420mm 16½" h x 550mm 21½" d
Body of oak, centre ring and neck tulipwood. Top, base and bands are goncalo alves. Received Grand Prize from New Rochelle New York Art Association 1989; first time in association's history the award was given to a work of art other than an oil painting

A teacher's inspiration can be a moving force. To artist/wood-turner George Radeschi, his wood shop teacher helped change his life.

'I was always interested in working with my hands,' says George, 'and my interest in wood was inspired by my high school wood shop teacher. He could do things with wood like no one else I've seen. I was fascinated by his abilities.'

Living the inspiration from his teacher every day, and from extensive study, during college and afterwards, of the history and art of ancient cultures, Radeschi has developed a technique through which he seeks to recapture the spirit of native American and ancient Egyptian, Roman and Grecian art.

He creates solid segmented turnings depicting the designs of ancient civilisations.

His vessels range in size from being appropriate for a credenza to being large enough for a child to stand in.

Some of Radeschi's turnings have centre rings, contrasting with the woods used in the body. Others have carefully designed patterns in equally precise proportions throughout the turning. Many of the designs begin near the bottom and run the height of the turning.

Imagery 380mm 15" h x
420mm 16½" d
Zebrawood, bubinga body; top
and base of walnut.
1st Place Award — Delaware
Art Museum, Wilmington,
Delaware, USA —
Contemporary Crafts
Exhibition 1987

Rings of Roses 735mm 29" h x
420mm 16½" d
Birch body, centre ring bird's
eye maple, rosewood, coco
bolo, goncalo alves; neck is
bubinga and goncalo alves on
bird's eye maple, goncalo alves
bands. Design 1990
Exposition, an architectural
and interior design exhibition
in Norfolk, Virginia, USA
(January-March 1990)

Odyssey 815mm 32" h x
500mm 19½" d
Walnut and black cherry
Fuller Museum of Art,
Brockton, Massachusetts, USA,
'Classicism Reconsidered'
exhibition February-May 1990.
Of 12 artists invited to
participate in exhibiting works
in the designs and motifs of
ancient Greek and Roman
cultures, Radeschi was the only
artist whose works are in wood

UNMISTAKABLE

Each turning takes scores of hours to complete as Radeschi's skills in design, mathematics, geometry, woodturning, joinery and finishing transform the natural colouring and grain of hundreds of solid pieces of native and exotic woods into striking combinations of patterns and shapes. The shapes vary but every one is a classic form arrived at from intensive research into the designs of pottery. Each one is distinctive and different, but all have Radeschi's unmistakable style. His turnings have been compared to a fine Persion rug with the inside looking exactly the same as the outside and finished in the same smooth patina.

Each angle is meticulously measured, each piece precision cut, glued together and turned on a lathe. Although each section of a turning is created individually and then joined with another for a final turning and shaping, all the sections must be calculated to fit almost perfectly together before they are joined for the final shaping. No clamps are used.

Lacquer is used for finishing, which is done on the lathe. By using the lathe, Radeschi can finish each piece much more easily and smoothly than if it were stationary.

The Brooklyn, New York, USA native has spent untold hours studying and experimenting with different cuts of woods, individually and with other woods, to see how each expands and contracts, how each reacts to different types of glues, to different humidity levels.

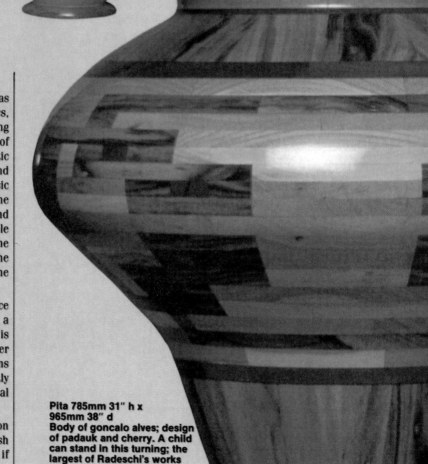

Pita 785mm 31" h x
965mm 38" d
Body of goncalo alves; design
of padauk and cherry. A child
can stand in this turning; the
largest of Radeschi's works

Crossroads 380mm 15" h x 355mm 14" d
Goncalo alves body, rosewood centre and neck, bubinga top and base. International Turned Object Show, Philadelphia, USA 1988

Sequoia 710mm 28" h x 560mm 22" d
Body red oak; centre ring rosewood, padauk and oak; neck rosewood on oak, base and top of bubinga

Turning Points 610mm 24" h x 440mm 17½" d
Body bubinga, top and base pearwood, centre ring rosewood and zebra wood, neck zebrawood
2nd Place Award — ArtQuest '88; New York, Philadelphia, Los Angeles. One of 36 chosen from 5000

STANDARDS

'There is no short cut to this method,' says Radeschi. The failure rate has been high. 'It's taken me nearly 30 years to reach this level. I'll still take a turning off a lathe and cast it aside if it doesn't meet my standards.' In fact, he keeps a less than perfect turning in his studio as a constant reminder of the pain it took to reach his present level.

Radeschi uses a variety of woods native to the northeastern states of the United States, such as maple, oak, walnut and birch. He also uses, but to a lesser degree, exotic woods.

Radeschi designs not only his turnings, but also the machinery with which to work. When he couldn't find a machine to meet a specific need in making the segmented turnings, Radeschi designed and built his own. He recently constructed a lathe larger than any on the market on which he can turn out even larger, more intricate vessels.

Radeschi constantly challenges himself. 'I have to leave my comfort zone, to try something I've never done before just to see how it will turn out.'

'One day, while I was at an art exhibition about native American pottery, I looked at a clay vessel and wondered if it could be done in wood.'

TESTIMONY

Radeschi's acceptance by museums, galleries and businesses is testimony that it could be done and done well. He first showed his segmented turnings at the Hudson River Museum in Yonkers, New York in 1987.

The following year he was one of 36 artists chosen from 5,000 to participate in ArtQuest '88 with exhibitions in New York, Philadelphia and Los Angeles. The jurors for the exhibition included curators of the Guggenheim Museum, the National Museum of Art, the Museum of Contemporary Art in Los Angeles, the San Francisco Museum of Modern Art and the Art Institute in Chicago. Radeschi's work received a second place award.

Also in 1988, he was selected to participate in the International Turned Objects Show in Philadelphia which featured the works of 116 turners from throughout the world.

Since then Radeschi's works have appeared in numerous exhibitions in the United States, including 'Classicism Reconsidered', an exhibition from February to May 1990 at the Fuller Museum of Art in the Boston suburb of Brockton, Massachusetts. Of the 12 artists invited to show works depicting the designs of ancient Rome and Greece, Radeschi was the only artist whose works were made of wood.

Despite his acclaim, Radeschi doesn't consider himself an artist. 'While it's very exciting to have the works accepted by the public and to receive recognition from museums and galleries, working with wood and especially creating these vessels is something I simply enjoy. It's the pride I have in a finished piece that motivates and satisfies me.' ■

Photos: Stephen Barth

The burl wood and irregular hardwoods which Michelle Holzapfel buys from loggers in woodlands near her Malboro, Vermont home she transforms into inventive and thought-provoking works of art, which reveal both herself and her environment.

Each piece retains the intrinsic elements of its organic nature. Wood vessels, bowls and still-life objects still bear the flaws and scars of time.

"There is nothing to be gained from filling the cracks or making believe they're not there," Michelle says. "I try to make a virtue out of what is there."

Even everyday objects she imbues with an inner beauty and spirituality. Her Roman Catholicism and mysticism have had a profound influence on the subjects she creates and the kinds of wood she chooses to work with.

These woods include lots of sugar maple, yellow and white birch, wild cherry and butternut.

Initially, she and her husband, David, a furniture maker, bought discarded and spalted wood because it was available and cheap. But they later discovered its true value, finding it "interesting and inspiring, not perfect, a matter of matching one's personality to the material."

Michelle prefers hardwoods, although she finds them challenging. Cherry, which is in plentiful supply near her, remains sharp through sanding, she says, and burls are hard. It is a sensual wood, smelling of roses, which polishes well.

Knitting Basket.

Going with th

SUSAN HALL

Michelle Holzapfel believes each piece of wood has personality and that what may be perceived as an imperfection can turn out to be a virtue. Here she tells Susan Hall about her mystical approach to wood craftsmanship.

Burls are caused by a tree virus and have a knobbly surface. They are more exciting to work with, says Michelle, because each piece is different.

Indeed, no two pieces of Michelle's work are alike, and she often names them after completion.

She has learned to work with the grain and not against it. Each piece has a personality of its own, she says. What can be perceived as an imperfection can turn out to be a virtue.

Her working style is flexible. She may conceive a design, then find a piece of suitable wood, but after cutting into it discover "a pocket, a crack, a knot, a hole in the surface, or a rotten area" which makes her alter her ideas, sometimes three or four times.

"Things go wrong in everyday life," she says. "You can't change the fabric of reality. The only chance is to modify your attitude towards things. It's a way of getting through life in general."

Applewoods is the name of the house and studio Michelle has shared for 17 years with her husband in a wooded, mountainous area of Vermont. They have two children, Simon, 20, and Forrest, 18. ▶

Michelle Holzapfel in her studio.

grain

Susan Hall is a freelance writer on art subjects.

She gained a bachelor's degree in art history from Moore College of Art and Design in Philadelphia.

Susan is also a photographer. She lives in Philadelphia.

Green Man Vase II 1992, maple
355mm 14" x 280mm 11"
100mm 4".

Their shop is open to the public from June until September. Behind it are three sheds where Michelle stores a huge supply of burls, all seasoning slowly, for five or six years, until she is ready for them.

Michelle believes all natural materials should be husbanded. She enjoys the self-sufficient aspects of her modest existence in the woodlands.

The home is important, she says, the place where we return to find our origins. "For a long time, the hearth and the altar were in one place, but in modern times, since the advent of organised religion, they have split from one another. Holiness and divinity should not be reserved for one day of the week, it infuses everything."

The technical qualities of her work are as simple and straight-forward as her lifestyle. And she tries to create an atmosphere of understanding and friendship through her work. The community is an essential part of her life.

From her parents she learned the tools for survival. Her mother, "a woman of outstanding patience," strongly influenced her creativity, while her father, a machinist, built a metal-worker's lathe which she converted for her own use, some 15 years ago, when she first began woodworking.

This lathe is capable of intricate work and is less stressful to use than an ordinary one. It operates on three different axes. Most lathes work on a central axis and dictate a style of woodturning with insides parallel to the outside. Michelle's turns around and spins horizontally.

The axes are in the wood and not in the tool. She can turn the wood on any of the axes, manipulating it with screw handles, left to right or in and out. It allows her to work for long stretches of eight or 10 hours a day.

Serpentine Vase is an example of two axes

turning and so is *Calla Leaves*, a pre-conceived idea for which Michelle found a suitable piece of wood.

It was the wood itself which inspired her to create *Persephone Vase*, an example of single axis turning.

Green Man Vase II has architectural elements, and the two faces were turned on the lathe. The design was carved out with a pencil grinder and some roughing out was done with a die grinder. The basic shape was inspired by an ancient Chinese ceramic.

The two opposing faces, portraying pleasure and displeasure, Michelle says express the dual nature in herself and her self-discovery.

While her lathe is adaptable to many interesting forms, Michelle ignores the unwritten rule of hollowing out vessels. She explained that the dominant mystique in woodworking has been centred on the technical skills required to turn a thin-walled, hollow vessel.

"For years this has seemed to be the essence of what woodturning is all about, the peak of its virtuosity. But for me this went across the grain. It leaves no room for heft, or weight, or substance. My pieces are not hollow, they're heavy. They also have surface carving, which takes a lot of effort, but to me the surface has meaning.

She doesn't design her vessels with the object of holding water. "Beauty is function" is how she describes their use. Many of her vessels have human features, such as faces, feet and shoulders.

She has been described by Albert LeCoff, the director of Philadelphia's Wood Turning Centre, as a sculptor rather than a turner.

Michelle refers to herself as a "woodworker" who does carving and turning. Over a year, she spends one month turning and the rest of the time carving.

The basic forms of her vessels she turns on the

Calla Leaves 1992, 280mm 11" x 305mm 12" x 125mm 5".

Persephone Vase 1992, white birch burl 240mm 9½" x 200mm 8" x 200mm 8".

Acorn Squash 1992, cherry burl 125mm 5" x 280mm 11" x 355mm 14".

Elemental Vase 1992, cherry burl 255mm 10" x 405mm 16" x 405mm 16".

Oak Leaves and Acorns Bowl 1992, walnut 200mm 8" x 355mm 14" x 315mm 12½".

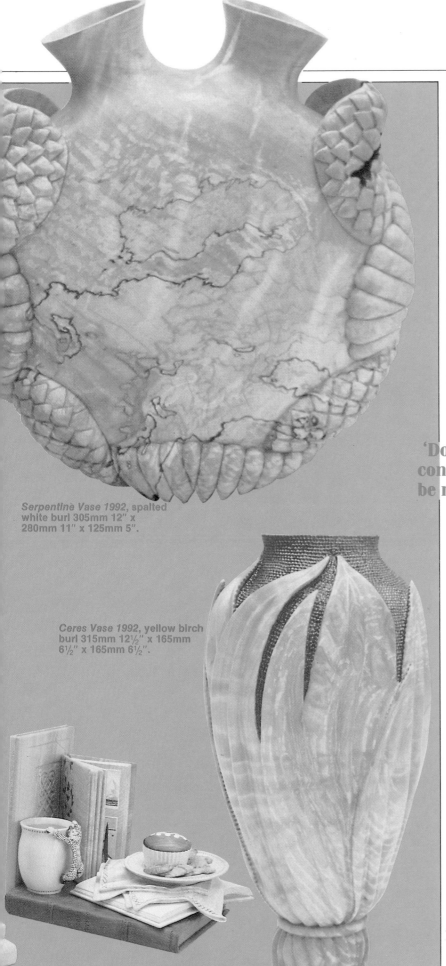

Serpentine Vase 1992, spalted white burl 305mm 12" x 280mm 11" x 125mm 5".

Ceres Vase 1992, yellow birch burl 315mm 12½" x 165mm 6½" x 165mm 6½".

Bookends 1992, yellow birch, cherry, birch and ash.

lathe, but most of the work involves the carving which follows. Some of this carving has reference to nature and the earth, a light, shiny surface contrasting with a dark and grainy one.

But it is not only vessels she carves. Still-lifes are another major feature of her work, often reflecting the tender, hidden (and to her, heroic) culture of domestic life.

"Domestic images have not been considered as worthy subjects to be made into art, but I think there are all kinds of things which can be said in art. I believe there's another kind of reality that deserves exposure."

Bookends is a classic example of her still life work based on a domestic theme. It was cut and carved in one piece with air-powered tools. The Raggedy Ann doll which forms part of it was shaped with a die grinder.

Michelle uses hand chisels and small files for fine detailed work and tight places.

Another of her 'domestic' works is a whimsical birthday cake with a slice removed.

'Domestic images have not been considered as worthy subjects to be made into art.'

Then there is her *Knitting Basket*, complete with balls of wool, half-finished knitting, glasses and scissors. The basket was turned as a bowl on the lathe and then carved into a basket shape with a pencil grinder. It was created in a variety of light and dark woods.

After the carving is completed, Michelle uses sandpaper braces to smooth surfaces before applying a coat of water, Watco, a Danish oil finish and Minwax, an antique oil finish.

She feels people value handmade objects more and more in a world where so many items are disposable.

Michelle, 41, continues her education at Marlboro College in Vermont. She originally studied mathematics but has concentrated more recently on mythology and religion, a continuing interest reflected in her wood creations.

She also studies woodturning, the roots of classical antiquity, and modern vessel forms. A keen drawer who at one time considered becoming a painter, art history and museums are among her interests.

Her work is on show in museums and galleries throughout the United States, and she writes and lectures on woodturning. Little of her work is sold on the wholesale market because it is chiefly one-of-a-kind. She sells her work through the Peter Joseph Gallery in New York City.

Michelle says success has not meant much to her. "There was no change in the way I felt. So I've just stopped thinking about it." ■

Tim Elliott was born in Alaska, spent a couple of years in England, but has lived most of his life in the eastern United States.

His first turning was done in school at the age of 12. The experience left him yearning to do more, but for more than 10 years he took no action beyond window shopping in machine-tool catalogues for hobbyist lathes.

Meanwhile, Tim completed his engineering education and took a job designing computer equipment – still his full-time occupation.

After marrying his wife, Karen, he confessed his secret desire to turn wood, and together they bought the cheapest lathe they could find.

Armed with half a dozen carbon-steel turning tools and no way to sharpen them, Tim happily reduced many a two-by-four down to shavings and kindling in his basement.

Several books and one new lathe later, he was just becoming confident enough to begin selling turnings when he discovered the local chapter of the AAW – the Central New England Woodturners.

Contact with this group accelerated the learning process and fanned his enthusiasm enormously.

His recent work has focused particularly on shapes. This article is one result of that process.

Success on a platter

TIM ELLIOTT

A step-by-step project on how to turn decorative platters on a faceplate, using an inside-out turning technique.

Inside-out turning is a widely known but little practised technique in which four square spindle blanks of equal size are combined to make a single large square blank of the same length, but twice as wide.

This is turned, leaving the ends square so that the pieces can be separated and re-assembled with the turned edges innermost, forming a hollow in the middle.

After turning, you are left with two solid ends connected by four posts, looking like a deformed hourglass.

After understanding how to make an inside-out spindle, I wondered whether the technique might be adapted for faceplate turning. It can. I quickly found I could make decorative platters in abstract flower shapes (FIG 1).

These pieces had a wonderful sculptural feeling, and contrasted well with my more conventional turned works. A letter published in *Woodturning* (Issue 8) confirmed my suspicion that I had 're-invented the wheel', but I think I've only just scratched the surface potential of this old technique. In this article, I'll describe my procedure, so you can try it too.

My platters are similar to a single end of an inside-out spindle, with the four corners corresponding to the four posts that would normally run the length of the spindle to the opposite end.

Some variety in shape is

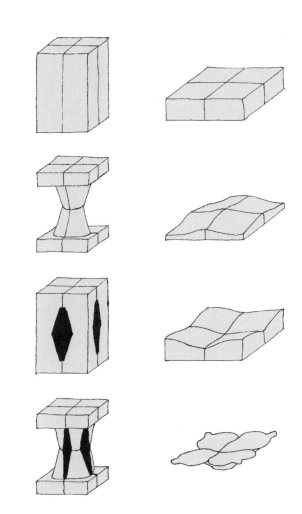

FIG 1 Inside-out turning between centres (left) compared to inside-out turning on a faceplate (right). The four pieces are each rotated 180 DEG between the second and third step shown

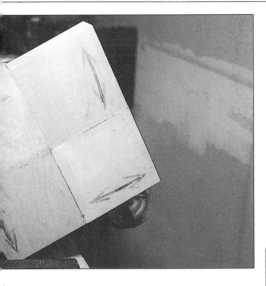

Photo 1 Four squares mounted for stage one of turning. Note the grain orientation relative to the toolrest.

Photo 2 Stage one turning complete.

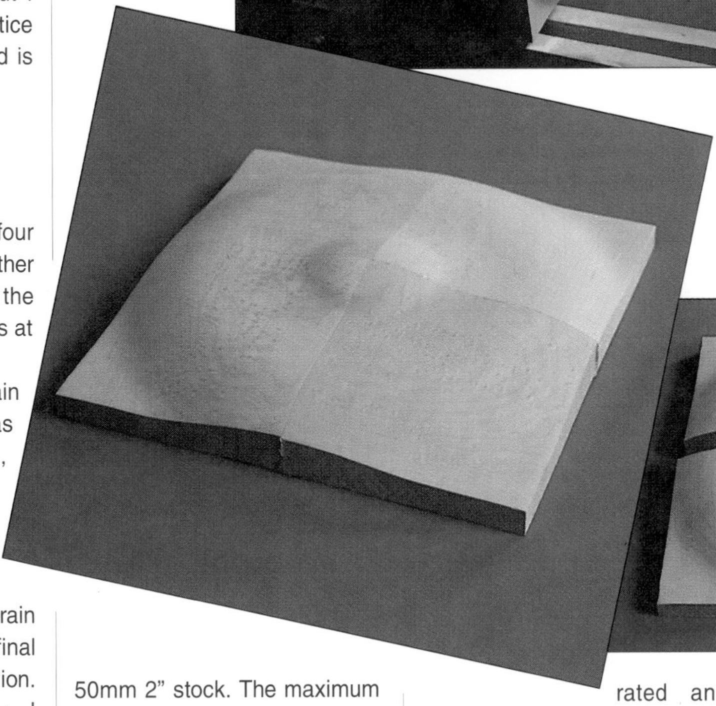

Photo 3 Detail showing contour of stage one

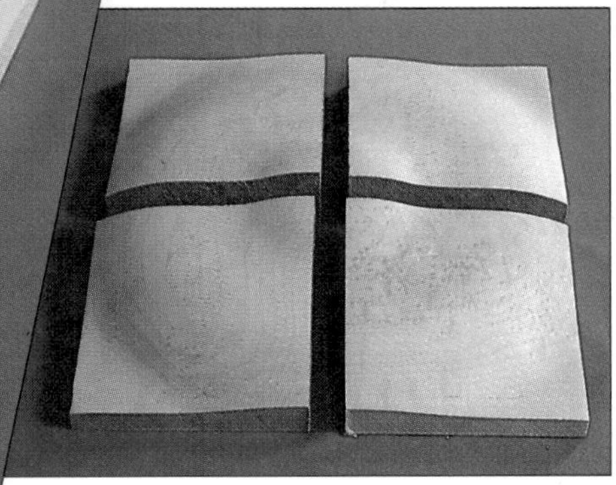

possible, but all will resemble four petalled flowers. Adventurous readers may like to extend the technique to get more, or less, petals: This is straightforward in theory, but I haven't attempted it in practice because the joinery needed is demanding.

Stage one: turning the top

The platter is made from four squares of wood glued together 'pinwheel' fashion, with the grain meeting at right angles at the seams (Photo 1).

This avoids weak end-grain to end-grain joints, but has limited my timber selection, as I prefer to avoid species such as zebrawood with strong linear colour patterns.

When glued up, such grain distracts the eye from the final shape, my main consideration. For the platter shown here, I have used birdseye maple.

Each square is cut from

to 400mm, nearly 16".

To find the maximum length of one side of the platter, divide by 1.4 to get 280mm 11". Dividing by two again tells me I must start with four squares at most 140mm 5½" on a side.

Once cut, glue the squares for stage one of turning with paper in the joints, to ease separation later. Remember to maintain end-grain to side-grain orientation at every joint. Even though they will be sepa-

50mm 2" stock. The maximum diameter of the finished platter is limited by the lathe bed (turning inboard). Mine can take up

rated and re-assembled later, the grain direction at this stage remains throughout the process.

I glue in stages, first making two rectangular sub-assemblies of two squares each, then combining them once the glue has set.

This takes longer than doing it all at once, but avoids having to apply pressure in two directions while trying to make all four squares meet in a single

point in the middle (FIG 2).

Hold this large square up to the headstock and picture it rotating with a gouge cutting into the corners as it turns. Note the gouge consistently meets either side-grain or end-grain at every corner.

If it meets side-grain, reverse the assembly as if the faceplate were mounted to the opposite face. Your imaginary gouge will now cut end-grain at the corners.

It seems against reason to ensure the worst possible grain orientation at this stage, but this allows cutting side-grain later when turning the bottom of what will then be a much thinner, more fragile piece.

Any tendency to tear out large chunks while cutting the corners at this stage of turning can be controlled by delicate use of a sharp tool – and by wrapping the edges of the work in heavy paper tape before starting the lathe. A reversible lathe or outboard tool rest would eliminate the problem entirely.

Having determined which

Photo 4 Stage one turning separated.

way to mount the work, screw the faceplate directly into the wood. The holes will be eliminated later when turning the bottom. Be careful to centre the work accurately.

The top surface of the platter is now turned (Photo 2) as if it were the bottom of a natural-edged bowl that happens to have a perfectly square rim (watch your fingers). The ▶

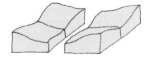

FIG 2 Gluing up four squares is easiest if done in two stages.

Photo 5 Square pieces re-oriented for stage two.

Photo 6 Detail showing contour of single square piece.

sanding, remove it from the lathe, and split the four squares (Photo 4) at the papered joints with chisel and mallet.

Stage two: turning the bottom

Rotate each square 180 DEG so the high points previously in the middle are now on the outside (Photo 5). This gives a roughly concave upper surface, our first hint of the final design. Photo 6 shows the contour of a single square piece.

Reglue the blocks in this new arrangement (Photo 7), but without the paper. You may need to trim the pieces with a sander for a tight fit.

Match the upper contours as closely as possible. Some hand sanding will probably be needed to smooth out bumpy joints at this stage.

Remount the platter with the flat side exposed for turning. Driving screws directly into the work is out of the question, as

desired shape will always be convex.

I suggest you experiment, but the shape I prefer is two-tiered (Photo 3). Be sure to leave the edges 10 to 20mm 3/8" - 3/4" thick all round, as these will be glued together to form the central joints in the completed piece.

After a quick

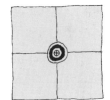

FIG 3 When mounting the platter to turn the bottom, the joints make it easy to centre the faceplate by eye. Turn the waste block round and cut a small hole in the centre with a gouge – then remove from the lathe and align to the joints.

Photo 8 The faceplate/waste block is mounted to work with hot-melt glue for stage two. Paper shims can be seen on the left.

Photo 7 Squares re-glued for stage two.

this would ruin the finished top.

Instead, I screw the faceplate to a waste block, quickly turn this true, then mount it to the platter using hot-melt glue (Photo 8 and FIG 3). This has good gap-filling properties but will still separate cleanly from the work once turning is completed.

Putting the assembly on the headstock, note the grain is now oriented so a gouge will

Photo 10 Stage two turning, with the tailstock in place for support.

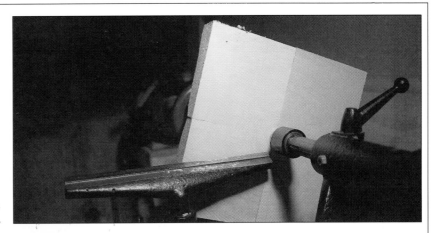

Photo 9 Stage two – note the grain orientation is opposite from stage one.

cut side-grain at the corners (Photo 9).

It's important to check the platter's top is mounted absolutely flat before starting to shape the bottom. The finished work will be thin and the petals must all be very close to the same thickness or one might be accidentally turned down to nothing.

To check flatness, I rotate the platter by hand until one corner just passes the toolrest. Then I hold a pencil against the toolrest so the point just touch-

▶

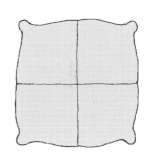

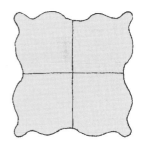

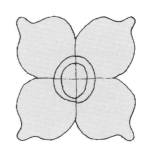

Photo 11 Stage two nearly complete, the outer shape emerging.

FIG 4 When turning the bottom, develop the final platter outline from the outer corners inward.

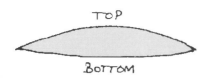

TOP

BOTTOM

FIG 5 Cross section of one 'petal.' The top will be more curved than the bottom. Blunt the sharp edges with sandpaper, but leave them thin to give a deceptively light and delicate feeling.

es the top side of the corner as it goes by.

Now, still rotating the platter by hand, the other three corners should also just touch the pencil point as they pass. If the work is not flat, correct it with paper shims between faceplate and waste block.

Turn the bottom, using the tailstock for support as long as possible (Photos 10 and 11). The process is like turning natural-edged bowls, in that the rim contains hollows which will surprise unwary fingers if you lose concentration.

This time, however, you won't keep the square rim square, and you must forget pre-conceived ideas about 'uniform wall thickness.'

The completed platter lies between two curved surfaces – the simple curve of the bottom and the more elaborate compound curve of the top

(Photos 12 and 13).

As it gets thin, the top contours will begin to intersect the bottom, naturally separating the four petals.

Each petal will in cross-section be thick in the middle, tapering down to sharp thin edges, like a well-worn piece of soap.

Work in stages from the outside rim to the centre, bringing each stage down to final thickness before moving inward (FIG 4).

The petals will taper to fine edges, which makes the overall shape sensitive to small amounts of material removed from the bottom.

This is a nuisance, in that the lathe must often be stopped to check the emerging shape – but it gives you a chance to creatively control the final result.

Later, this thin edge gives the finished piece a deceptively fragile feel when handled, but the thickness at the centre of each petal will reassure you if you need it at this point (FIG 5).

It may be necessary to break away some paper-thin debris from the edges as you work to see what shape you are really getting.

Finish-sand the bottom with the lathe stopped. I use this moment to gently round over the sharp edges and make any slight adjustments that might be needed to get a pleasing symmetrical outline for the piece as a whole.

The hot-melt glue separates more easily if it is first frozen. Put the faceplate and platter together into the freezer and forget them for a couple of hours.

This makes the joint brittle, so I can normally remove the faceplate from the platter with a couple of firm but glancing mallet blows (on the faceplate).

Touch up the sanding and apply your favourite finish. Enjoy! ●

Photo 12
The finished work, top.

Photo 13
The finished work, side

David Ellsworth cutting logs with the chainsaw for the students.

John Hunnex was a professional photographer for 35 years, and has been turning wood for 33 years.

He started his working life as a local newspaper photographer, and progressed to studio work, photographing elegant homes and artists' work. He eventually set up his own studio and staged exhibitions of his photography.

In 1966 he became a lecturer in photography at Goldsmith's College School of Art in South London. He stayed for 17 years and became Senior Lecturer before taking early retirement following a heart attack.

He learned woodturning at school and returned to the craft as a hobby. On retirement the hobby became his full-time occupation.

John specialises in bowls and vessels and enjoys working with a wide variety of woods, trying always for the unusual.

John has held several solo and joint gallery exhibitions and has had his work published in magazines. He is a member of both the AWGB and the AAW. He has his home and workshop at Woodchurch in Kent.

Vilas Diwadkar straddles the lathe, Ellsworth fashion.

THE ELLSWORTH EXPERIENCE

JOHN HUNNEX

It's never too late to learn says John Hunnex as he spends a few days with *Woodturning's* American Adviser learning his tricks of the trade.

When I recently got the opportunity to spend some time with David Ellsworth, one of the accepted masters of woodturning, I jumped at the chance.

It came about when an American businessman friend invited me and a friend over for a holiday, which would include a three-day workshop course at the Ellsworth School of Woodturning at Quakertown, Pennsylvania.

To structure the course to our needs, David sent us a questionnaire asking about our level of experience and what we wanted to learn. He also asked us to take photographs of our work with us.

I said I wanted to learn how to use the specialist tools he had developed for his hollow form turning, for which he has gained international recognition.

David limits the workshop to four students so the specific needs of each individual can be ►

addressed. On this course there were two Americans — David Crawford (our host) and Vilas Diwadkar, plus David Bates and myself from Kent. We were the first UK turners to attend, though I am sure we won't be the last!

David told us the focus would be on developing small and large scale bowls and vessels — from salad bowls to hollow forms — using both faceplate and between-centre techniques.

Subjects would include basic and advanced applications of traditional and non-traditional tool design, principles of sharpening, refinement of tool usage, foam-back sanding, finishing, object photography and methods of work. Particular emphasis would be placed on object design, reading grain patterns within the raw materials, exploring our design potential and discovering methods of personalising the objects we made.

We started on Thursday evening with an informal introductory meeting in David and Wendy Ellsworth's beautiful home and gallery, which was designed by David, showing his particular creative flair. The house is set in a 20-acre woodland site (plenty of practice timber!)

I felt I had been allowed into Aladdin's cave! I was surrounded by pottery, furniture, carvings and turnings by internationally recognised craftsmen, including a piece by David Pye.

The combination of designer furniture and artefacts had nevertheless been blended into a home in the real sense of the word. Even some of the kitchen utensils were a craftsman's delight. It was a collector's dream!

We were also taken into the workshop to familiarise us with the layout. David is, of course, conscious of health and safety in the workshop. To this end, he has designed and built an ingenious system of dust extraction which removes dust while retaining heat.

He has also installed an air compression system with three service points strategically placed to serve the working lathes. This is a good system for blowing out cuttings and dust from hollow forms — even when the hole is only 6mm ¼" wide.

It also served to clear the dust from the workshop before starting work. David goes around in the morning blowing the dust from all the places it builds up. With his extractor running it leaves a dust-free workshop.

The lathes available to us were two Generals (260), a Delta Rockwell, a Jim Thompson custom-built lathe with 760mm 30" DIA capacity, and a Woodfast Shortbed.

There were Henry Taylor Superflute gouges, the Thompson Swing-Tip deep cutting tools, and David's own angled tools for our use. It was a typical professional workshop with some of David's work in progress. This was great to see.

There were also some pieces with a layer of dust telling us they had been discarded at the moment, maybe because the wood was faulty, with those little annoyances that trees put in to get back at us! Even so, the pieces would still have graced a gallery or a home, but David's standards are so high that he has to be brutal in what he can pass as worthwhile. This must be one of the disadvantages of being one of the best turners around.

The tools were something else. Some of them were made by David himself for his own particular needs, but he was still prepared to share his knowledge with us.

I knew that this was not the kind of course where you were set five projects and went home proudly clutching five items! This was to be a total learning experience relating to our own turning potential, and I looked forward with great anticipation to my first day's work.

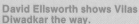
Photos: John Hunnex.

David Ellsworth shows Vilas Diwadkar the way.

Day 1 started at the chalkboard, followed by a discussion and demonstration of cutting the log. We then looked at choosing the position of the wood on the lathe to get the best out of it. If the wood was to be used for a hollow form, we positioned it so that the pith ran parallel.

We then placed the wood between centres, turned a ball, reversed it, and decided whether the ball should become two bowls or a hollow form. We spent some time looking at cutting techniques. In the afternoon we got on a lathe and started to put into practice what we had learned in the morning.

We also looked at stance at the lathe. David is of course known for his straddle over the bed — actually sitting on the lathe — but we also looked at standing at the lathe, both inside (on the Thompson) and outside on the others. He emphasised that body alignment and movement were vital elements in the turning process.

David was constantly on hand to help us get started on our chosen pieces, particularly with the use of the special tools. He was looking at the movement of our wrists, hands and elbows as part of the process.

David Ellsworth discusses one of his Solstice series with Vilas Diwadkar, David Crawford and David Bates.

David Ellsworth with two of his home-made tools.

As David had work included we were all invited to attend and saw some outstanding furniture, turnings and glass.

On our third and final day we went straight into the workshop to either continue with previous work or to start a fresh piece. If at any time we needed advice, David was on hand to support.

If you needed a graphic, rather than verbal explanation, then over we went to the chalkboard until David felt you had grasped the point he was trying to make. This was particularly important when turning blind inside a small hole in a hollow form! His ability to explain himself showed what a good teacher he was.

We were taken to his spacious photo studio above his workshop and taught how to photograph the work we produced, and make inexpensive lighting units.

We then had a valuable discussion about David's latest work — including his *Solstice* series. He continued to stress the importance of design, shape and form, and the inner deeper feeling the craftsman should have for his work

> 'Like all good craftsmen he made it all look easy, but he didn't hide any secrets. This is a craftsman who is not in fear of competition, however small or large.'

when turning. We were hearing his philosophy on turning which was most absorbing.

We talked about the physical stress of turning and he showed us a bar hanging from the ceiling of his workshop to enable him to hang on and stretch tired limbs and loosen up tense muscles.

Like all good craftsmen he made it all look easy, but he didn't hide any secrets. In fact I found he really wanted you to learn. This is a major sign of a craftsman who is not in fear of competition, however small or large.

Our final teaching session was back to the lathes to complete work and each student was taken aside individually and shown how to sharpen a Henry Taylor Superflute Gouge in David's own particular way, and also the angle tool of his own design. We were all given the opportunity to ask him about sharpening any other tool we wished to know about.

David managed to achieve all he had set out to do in the prospectus — quite an achievement with a variety of students.

Then all too soon it was time to go. I wished I could have stayed for a longer course, but after we said our goodbyes we all know we were much better off for going through 'The Ellsworth Experience'.

With the help of his follow-up sheets and other information, I am going to try to prove to David that all his hard work was not in vain. ■

On Day 2 we were reminded of what we had already done. What had happened so far was just part of the total learning process and we were encouraged then to start another piece of work putting into practice the techniques.

After lunch David gave a critique of students' work from the slides and photographs we had taken. He showed an astute understanding of the illustrations produced and stressed the importance of design. He also said that technique should not be allowed to get in the way of design.

He always emphasised the positive aspects of work first and then gently explained where he thought we had gone wrong, so his words registered in our minds with the nicest possible impact. This is the best way to offer a critique without making enemies!

We spent some time looking at tool sharpening, with particular reference to the tool bits of the Thompson tool.

There was an extra bonus in store for us that evening with a private view of an exhibition in a local gallery (part of The Trenton Museum) called *The Forest Refined* showing the work of master craftsmen in wood and glass.

Turn a hollow pot

JULES TATTERSALL

"How do you get inside?" is a question most asked of Jules about his narrow-opening hollow pots. Here he gives some answers.

One of the questions most asked of me at shows and exhibitions of my work is "How do you get in there?" — referring to the process of hollowing a vessel through a small aperture.

In this article I hope to answer some of the questions that arise by running through the basic techniques I use to turn a pot.

It should be said that there are many ways of achieving a result in most crafts, and turning wood is no exception. My methods are by no means hard and fast rules, but like many professional turners, the need to produce work efficiently and quickly often causes me to stick with what I know and find comfortable.

Though the piece shown in this project is a smallish elm burr pot, much larger pieces can be turned using more or less the same techniques, with larger tools and good strong fixings being the order of the day.

The first step of any turning operation is to select the blank most suitable for the required project. In this case, a pot, the blank needs to have some depth in relation to width.

If you are to avoid a flattish vessel then depth should be a little greater that width, allowing for the spigot and a good full shape to the piece.

Bark inclusions must be noted, and experience will allow you to know if they will ruin or indeed enhance the pot. Unless I am doing a natural opening to the piece I ensure the area around the intended rim of the pot is free of bark inclusions, shakes, etc.

With this in mind I mount the blank between centres with the intended top towards the drive and bottom toward the tailstock (Photo 1).

Photo 1 Mounting the blank.

With the piece rotating, I rough out the basic shape using a 20mm ¾" roughing out gouge. At the same time as creating the basic pot shape, I turn a

Photo 2 Basic pot shape turned, with dovetail spigot.

dovetail spigot to fit the Axminster 4-jaw dovetail chuck (Photo 2).

For smaller pots you can use other spigot chucks, but where possible I use the 4-jaw because the spigot does not have to be accurately measured. This saves time which is vital when doing batches of work.

I now mount the piece on the chuck, and any slight wobbles are 'fine turned' away. I find the 4-jaw chuck so accurate that the piece generally mounts perfectly symmetrically.

It is then power sanded with a coarse grit to remove any torn grain, etc (Photo 3).

Photo 3 Power sanding removes torn grain.

Photo 4 Cutting grooves with a small spindle gouge.

If the pot is to have a smooth surface I continue the sanding process through the grits to 400. However, as this one is to be ribbed, I begin the grooving using a small spindle gouge (Photo 4).

The grooves are turned as far down the pot as is safe without fouling the chuck (Photo 5). **This is very important — if you are not familiar with using these chucks keep knuckles, fingers and sleeves well away.**

Photo 5 The grooves are cut as far as is safe.

Photo 6 Wire brushing gives a nice texture.

I use a rotating wire brush to finish the surface. The texture this gives the grooves appeals to me and it's easier than sanding between them (Photo 6).

Using a skew chisel on its side I create a centre vee, which will help to guide the centre bore (Photo 7).

For boring the centre I use an auger with handle. This technique can be a little difficult to get used to and if you have

Photo 7 A centre vee helps guide the centre bore.

Photo 8 A peg depth gauge on the borer.

other methods of boring which work well then my advice is to stick with them. However my method is quick and quite accurate.

A peg provides a good depth gauge (Photo 8) or you could use tape. With the machine running slowly the boring tool is pushed in (Photo 9).

Very soon it may bite and start to be pulled in of its own accord. After 25mm 1″ or so of travel I pull the borer back to clear shavings, otherwise it can get very tight and want to spin with the lathe. It also becomes difficult to pull out.

I repeat this all the way down to the point where the peg is about to touch the pot rim, and then once again pull the borer out.

Two important safety tips should be noted when boring freehand:

1) It sometimes takes a good strong pull to remove the borer, and so it is important to remove the tailstock centre from the tailstock unless you want a visit to casualty sporting a new elbow accessory.

2) Have good access to the stop switch, as you should have for **all** turning operations. If the borer should bite too much to pull free, stopping the machine will prevent you boring through the base of the pot and maybe into the neighbour's garage.

Armed now with the skew chisel on its side acting as a ▶

Jules Tattersall is a professional woodturner who lives and works in Anglesey, North Wales.

After leaving college in 1978, where he studied social geography, Jules travelled the world and had many and varied jobs, including aircraft pilot.

He became involved in woodturning in 1983 while living in Australia where he was inspired by the work of Richard Raffan. He returned to the UK four years later and settled in Anglesey where he went to school and where his family still live.

Since then he has run his own business and has had his work included in many shows, exhibitions, galleries and quality shops throughout the UK, Europe and the USA.

Jules Tattersall, Stanley Mill Cottage, Mill Lane, Trearddur Bay, Anglesey LL65 2BZ. Tel: 0407 861294

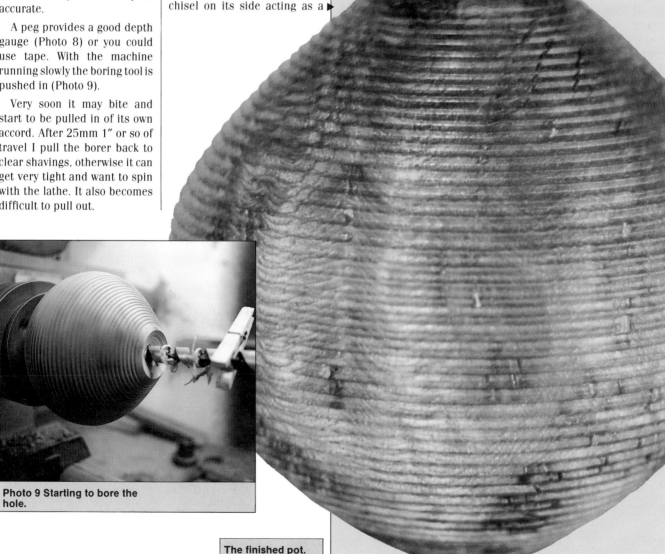

Photo 9 Starting to bore the hole.

The finished pot.

Photo 10 Using the skew as a scraper to start the hollowing.

scraper, I open up the area around the centre hole (Photo 10).

People always seem to frown on scrapers, suggesting they are inferior tools to the gouge or cutting tools. I make no distinction when turning and would happily send in a team of wood-eating piranha fish, if such beasts existed, if I thought they would do the job.

If the pot does not have too acute an angle or corners difficult to get at, I will do most of the hollowing with the bowl gouge in the same way as I would turn out the hollow of any

Photo 11 Continuing with a bowl gouge.

Photo 12 Much of the hollowing is done by feel.

bowl (Photo 11). You will have to experiment with angles and different bevels, as much of this turning is done by feel (Photo 12).

For much larger pots I would use a combination of large bowl gouges and Stewart system type tools.

Photo 13 A cranked tool is ideal for getting inside.

Photo 14 Getting into the corners.

Some tools I make myself. A cranked tool (Photo 13) is ideal for pots with curves too difficult to get at with the gouge, and also for cleaning the inside of the pot after the gouge has done all it can (Photo 14).

One of the difficulties with any hollowing operation is the

removal of shavings. Working with burrs it isn't so much shavings as bits, but either way they soon clog the pot and need to come out.

Vacuums can be partially successful but if the opening is quite small I tend to use the 'take the thing off the lathe and shake it around a lot' technique. I make sure to remove it with the chuck still attached to the pot in case it won't re-align well.

Using a combination of the above tools I complete the hollowing process checking the wall thickness occasionally with double-ended callipers (Photo 15).

Photo 15 Checking the wall thickness with callipers.

I next sand the rim of the pot and as much of the inside of the rim as is safe without fingers being caught. I then remove it from the chuck.

I keep a ready supply of scrap blanks to hand as friction chucks, and mounting one onto the 4-jaw chuck I turn down a spigot to the same size as the pot opening (Photo 16).

After checking the fit (Photo 17) I take a further

Photo 16 A blank is turned to the same size as the pot opening.

Photo 17 Checking for fit.

Photo 18 Cloth or paper towel gives a good friction fit.

shaving off to allow for cloth or paper towel between the pot and spigot. A good fit (not too tight or the pot will crack) will drive the piece when pressure is applied from the tailstock (Photo 18).

The dovetail on the pot is now turned down and the profile of the pot continued to a point at which the base is decided upon (Photo 19). I add the few remaining grooves and wire brush as before. The last 12mm ½" or so of pot is sanded.

Photo 19 Now the base can be turned.

Photo 20 The base spigot is turned as far as possible.

The base is trued and cut until just a small knob is left at the tailstock centre (Photo 20) and this is removed by hand (Photo 21). With experience it is possible to cut the knob away completely on the lathe but a visor is recommended in case it becomes airborne.

Photo 22 The base is sanded.

Photo 23 A final buff on the lathe after oiling and waxing.

I now sand the base either by hand or using a small power disc (Photo 22). Once again, with experience and a good fit between pot and chuck it is possible to do this on the lathe, though not safely with larger pieces.

I finish the piece with a couple of coats of Danish oil and a final coat of beeswax prior to a final buffing using a buffing brush on the lathe (Photo 23).

There is my pot (Photo 24). All I have to do now is sell it — and all the others too! ∎

Photo 21 The final knob is removed by hand.

"I would happily send in a team of wood-eating piranha fish if I thought they would do the job."

THE BIG TIME

Ainslie Pyne, a wood sculptor, lived in New Zealand before moving to Adelaide, South Australia, in 1968.

An Arts and Crafts course in the late 1970s introduced her to wood as a medium.

She volunteered, in 1984, to carve a lifesize mermaid figurehead for the South Australian sail training ship *One and All*.

President of the South Australian Woodgroup Inc. for the past four years (and re-elected for a fifth), she also edits the group's newsletter, which is exchanged by many groups throughout New Zealand and Australia.

Her seven week stay in New Zealand has led to a proposed visit by South Australian woodworkers to Christchurch and Nelson.

In 1992, Ainslie helped stage an Adelaide exhibition of woodcarvings, sculpture and marquetry showing endangered species, to raise money for the World Wildlife Fund.

It was judged by UK Woodcarver Ian Norbury, whose Australian and New Zealand tour Ainslie organised.

Dan Cunningham is a woodturner on a giant scale, some of his blanks weighing as much as a small car. He also turns fast, spinning these huge blocks of wood at a suicidal 600 RPM.

He is one of a number of artists who have set up home and workshop in the Nelson area of New Zealand's South Island. Dan and his family moved there from Hawaii when their health began to deteriorate after volcanic eruptions emitted poisonous gases.

They were also fed up with Hawaii's over-crowding — and lack of wood — choosing New Zealand because of the more leisurely lifestyle, the pleasant climate, its Polynesian history and timber resources.

Soon after his arrival in the Nelson area, Dan, 39, joined the local Guild of Woodworkers, and it was at the guild's annual exhibition that I was introduced to him.

He was showing a koa bowl which intrigued everyone because of its round bottom. We all wondered how it was supposed to sit on a flat surface.

We met again later at his home, on a guided tour of prominent guild members I was given by the Nelson guild's past-president, Wilson Hawke. There I learnt more of Dan's background.

AINSLIE PYNE

Dan Cunningham is a woodturner who thinks BIG and lives dangerously, turning huge blocks of wood at high speed. Ainslie Pyne visited him at his North Island New Zealand workshop.

Norma with 'the world's biggest bowl.'

He originally hails from Lancaster, Ohio, USA, and started turning in 1978 after quitting college. Later that year he moved to Hawaii on the advice of a friend, where he met his wife to be, Norma.

Now they have settled into a small acreage near Riwaka, a country town on the Western shores of Tasman Bay, with their daughter Ohela, 12, and son, Dane, 10, who turns regularly on his Klein lathe.

Wilson and I were amazed at the size of the various pieces of lathe equipment in Dan's workshop.

He turns on a huge lathe, capable of holding a bowl six feet (two metres) in diameter. The faceplates have 18 bolts attaching them to the blank, while the biggest toolrest looks like a harvester's scythe.

The lathe, which Dan designed, has a 63mm 2½″ headstock shaft riding on two extra-heavy-duty pillow block bearings. These are mounted on a 25mm 1″ steel plate 610mm 24″ x 305mm 12″ and welded to steel bars for anchors in the solid 915mm x 915mm 36″ x 36″ column which is poured around the steel superstructure.

The bed is six foot (two metres) long, and it is 915mm 36″ from the middle of the headstock shaft to the surface of the bed, which is made from hot and cold laminated steel to eliminate vibration.

The tailstock was amazing to behold. Seven foot long (2130mm) and about nine inches (230mm) in diameter, it looked more like a nuclear missile head than part of a woodturner's lathe.

The lathe's total capacity is six foot (2 metres) in diameter, the same in depth, with a weight capacity of 1500 kg. The 5 hp motor is fixed on the floor and to give the required torque, drives through a Hyster forklift transmission with four speeds in high and low options controlled through a variable speed option.

Dan said it cost him $1700 just to dismantle the lathe for his move to New Zealand, taking four days with jackhammers to remove from its concrete pillars set into the floor.

Apart from the lathe, the main items of equipment in his workshop are a 355mm 14″ bandsaw, a one-ton capacity crane for lifting blocks of wood into position, a 20 cfm air compressor, an oil tank (or vat) and three chainsaws. His sanding is done with air tools.

One piece of equipment a lot of Australian chainsaw carvers would love to have is what Dan calls a 'canoe carver' — a steel cylinder with chainsaw chain wrapped round it like a barber's pole, which enables you to make a 100mm 4″ wide cut.

It rips surplus wood away faster than a dozen or so Arbortech blades lined up side by side. Deadly! ▶

Dan finds a suitable burl.

Back at the workyard.

A large faceplate is attached with 18 bolts.

Norma with mango bowl 585mm 23″ H x 915mm 36″ DIA on a turned base.

Several twisted trunks were standing in a corner of the workshop. Dan explained they were from a distant cousin of New Zealand's rata tree, which is called ohia in Hawaiian. Their twisted trunks looked like the columns in St Peter's basilica in Rome.

Dan is a collector of rare species of the world's timber, with a stack of these treasures. He has a broad knowledge of the evolution of forest timbers from the whole Pacific region.

I admired a large billet of sandalwood and an equally large piece of lignum vitae, much bigger than the sample-sized pieces most collectors possess.

He also has a mountain of New Zealand red beech burls to turn and is keen to work on large sections of radiata pine. With his finishing methods this should come up as well as Norfolk Island pine.

Other timbers he uses include monkey pod tree, Norfolk Island pine, acacia koa (which is similar to Tasmanian blackwood but with a more showy fiddleback figure), mango, Japanese criptomaria, and eucalyptus saligna (bluegum).

He also has a long list of contacts to supply him with large logs and burls from New Zealand's temperate rainforests, many of them found on the forest floor, having been rejected as good saw logs.

Dan invited us into his home to see photographs of work he had made in Hawaii, one showing a large koa bowl owned by the actor Richard Chamberlain.

Another bowl belongs to Paul Simon, of Simon and Garfunkel fame, while actor James Stewart also has one. Others are on display in large corporations.

Dan admits to having had the good fortune to build up a large clientele. "Rather than trying to promote myself among woodturners, I have promoted myself among buyers of art. So I am well known to corporations and collectors, but virtually unknown to woodturners."

Most of the bowls are very large, big enough for his two children to sit in side by side. To make them even more impressive, Dan turns pedestal-like display stands or has stands made by a joiner to complement them.

He uses a traditional Hawaiian method of repairing cracks and splits in his bowls — stitching the two sections together. The more stitching a bowl has, the more value as a collector's item in Hawaii.

Earlier, I had asked Dan about his entry in the guild's annual exhibition, the round bottomed bowl. Was it to ensure a salad was well-tossed?

He explained that because Hawaiians had no clay to make their household utensils they had developed wooden bowls instead. These would have been cushioned by the sandy floor of a hut,

A hydraulic crane lifts the blank into place.

The headstock is attached.

Now the tailstock.

their rounded bottom only becoming a problem after European settlers introduced flat topped surfaces such as tables to the island. Small rings of plaited vines were then made as seats for the bowls. Norma is trying to make these from New Zealand flax.

Dan showed us photographs to illustrate his turning procedure. Starting, say, with a 520kg 1000lb piece of walnut, he roughs it down as round as he can with a chainsaw.

A small tractor takes the log to the lathe, where a large faceplate is bolted on, ranging in size from 180mm 7" DIA to 610mm 24" DIA.

> 'The tailstock was amazing to behold . . . It looked more like a nuclear missile head than part of a woodturner's lathe.'

The partly trued blank is lifted into place with a hydraulic crane, the headstock and tailstock attached, the set-bolt set, and, after a little more chainsaw trimming on the bottom of the bowl, the piece is ready for turning.

In keeping with the rest of his equipment, Dan's turning chisels are large and of his own design. He obtains HSS shafting, has it milled to his required shape, slides it inside a length of galvanised tubing, locks it with a set screw and finds he has all the weight, strength and leverage needed.

The toolrest is 286mm 11¼" steel shaft bent 90 DEG so it can be swung where required.

Ready for turning.

Turning begins on the exterior.

Now the interior.

Norfolk Island pine bowl 635mm x 635mm 25" x 25".

A central support column is removed as late as possible.

Dan turns many different types of wood at a faster speed than Ed Moulthrop's 50 RPM, a speed fine, Dan says, for softer woods, "which turn like butter," but not for hardwoods.

These, he says, would not even cut at those revs, so he speeded up. First the block is turned at 300 RPM to close to the finished shape.

As it is now balanced the tailstock is retracted and the speed increased to 500-600 RPM to attack the inside of the bowl. "So it's turned quick. That's how I achieve a good cut. There's an incredible wind comes off the turning."

Asked about the possibility of the lathe wandering when turning large pieces of wood at such high speeds (wood not reasonably balanced and true, with a fair amount still to be chewed off it), Dan said the lathe couldn't walk as it was held by solid concrete pillars sunk 1525mm 5' into the floor. He estimates there is about 20 tons of concrete anchoring the lathe to the floor.

The headstock is a metre (39") above the bed of the lathe, but Dan does not need a platform to stand on when turning, because he will have the bed of the lathe set lower.

"You should look down at a slight angle into the inside of the bowl. I like the headstock spinning right at my solar plexus," he said.

First he turns the exterior, then the interior, leaving a central column for support as late as possible before removing. "You have to remember that if one of these flies off I'm a dead man. There's no fooling around with this."

He turns from one side only, not from the back of the lathe. "The live centre passes right under my arm. I kind of rest on the live centre."

Dan does all his turning with custom-made gouges, rarely using scrapers. He keeps a sharp edge to his tools with his grindstone mounted one step away.

Curiously, and contrary to popular opinion, he operates with a convex shaping to his tools. But the large clean cut shavings prove its effectiveness. Dan sharpens some tools 20-25 times a day, on average. ▶

The completed walnut bowl is big enough to take Dan's children Dane and Ohelo.

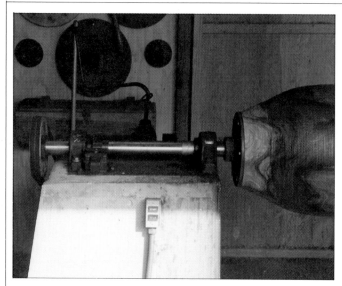

When the walls are down to about 292mm 11½" and the dead weight considerably reduced, the outer ring of coach screws are removed and the bottom and outside of the bowl are given a final shaping, leaving some sap wood to give a contrast to the darker heart wood and a rounded base to the bottom, as on a Hawaiian bowl.

Removed from the faceplate, the bowl then spends up to six months in a kiln used to control

A smaller bowl on the giant lathe.

Display stands are made to complement large bowls.

Dan tackles the exterior again. Note the handy grinder, and monster faceplates on the wall.

Now for the interior.

'If one of these flies off I am a dead man. There's no fooling around with this.'

the drying and dehumidifying before final shaping.

For sanding and finishing operations Dan uses a variety of air operated tools but two in particular — a lathe and an air compressor.

Good sandpaper, he says, is hard to come by. He uses one normally used for sanding cars, which cannot become clogged. "It's very expensive, but excellent for woodworking."

Small items he sands on the lathe or in his lap, but this is not always possible with larger pieces. These he turns down to the finished thickness and places on a bean bag to sand with the air tools.

Dan also uses a wet rag sanding technique which he thinks all woodturners should learn because it gives an improved finish. He explained how it works:

"After you have done your rough grit sanding, take a very damp wash cloth and wipe the surface of the wood. This will bring up the nap and any bruising."

Then he sands it again with rough grit, wipes it down and repeats the job while the wood is still wet.

After sanding has been completed, passing through several grades of grit, bowls are given an oil bath for up to 72 hours in a large stainless steel vat.

This is filled with equal parts of raw linseed oil, mineral turpentine and satin polyurethane mixture heated to about blood temperature (100 DEG F).

After removal from the vat, they are placed at an angle to allow excess oil to drip off and the surface oil to set.

Dan says his method of immersing the bowls in the oil bath and leaving them for a time allows the finish to penetrate right through the bowl, bringing out the natural beauty of the wood.

The hard work then begins, with Dan rubbing down the surface with steel wool, removing just under a millimetre of wood.

After a day in the workshop handling huge blocks of wood, how does Dan relax?

"The whole family goes into a ritual of rubbing me," he says. "I lie on the floor and a kid gets on each leg while Norma climbs on my back and they work me back into shape. It's horrible, like a Japanese massage." ■

The kiln drying room where part-turned bowls are left to season for up to six months.

A WOMAN'S WAY

NIGEL GARDNER

One of the few British female woodturners talks of the advantages and disadvantages of being a woman in a man's world.

The Space Within,
14 Star Brewery
Workshops,
Castle Ditch Lane,
Lewes,
East Sussex BN7 1YJ.

Rose-Marie Yeh was born in Countesthorpe, Leicestershire, in 1964. Her father is Chinese and her mother English.

Educated to A level standard in Art and Design, she took a foundation course in those subjects at Leicester Polytechnic before studying for a BA (Hons) in Wood, Metal, Ceramics and Plastics at the University of Brighton.

After graduating, she opened a workshop in Lewes, East Sussex, with a grant from the Prince's Youth Business Trust, and expanded last year to a retail shop selling her decorative hardwood bowls.

Artistically, she sees herself fitting between two cultures — East and West. She aims through her work to get in touch with the inner spiritual being.

A visit to China and Hong Kong in 1979 stimulated an interest in Taoism which permeates her work.

She has studied Tai Chi for more than two years and is fascinated by growing Bonsai trees and Alpine plants.

In the short term she wants to develop her ideas, but sees travel abroad, perhaps in China or Japan, as a necessary part of her future development, to gain a deeper insight into the Eastern side of her culture.

Bowls in (top to bottom) eucalyptus burr, olive, walnut, spalted beech, eucalyptus burr and spalted sycamore.

Rose-Marie Yeh, one of only a few British female woodturners, has found her femininity an advantage rather than the reverse. She is, for example, never short of advice. "Men keep coming into the shop and telling me how to do things," she says.

She feels most men take woodturning too seriously, worrying about matters such as whether tools are sharpened perfectly and whether they are doing something correctly. "I don't care, provided the end result is right," she says.

Because of this fundamental difference in the way women look at these things, Rose-Marie feels it gives them more freedom to be creative. "You have to be true to yourself and do it your way."

While she accepts that some women in a man's world feel the need to be better than men in order to be accepted by them, she thinks most women approach things from a different perspective.

"I hope it makes my pieces more sensitive than men's," she says.

Even some women who come into the shop are surprised at finding a women woodturner. "Did you make these?" they will ask.

Rose-Marie admits, however, there are times when it would be nice to have the support of other women woodturners. "I went to one of the Loughborough conferences and there were five women and about 200 men."

She would like to establish a women turners' group in the South East, to possibly meet up with a similar group in Cambridge.

Rose-Marie says she faced no parental opposition when she told them she wanted to be a professional turner, although her Chinese father had "wanted me to become a housewife, or an engineer," his profession.

It was school which first introduced Rose-

▶

'Even some women who come into the shop are surprised to find a woman woodturner. "Did you make these?" they will ask.'

Rose-Marie Yeh in her previous studio/workshop at the Star Brewery Workshops.

Top, myrtle burr bowl, 230mm 9" DIA x 125mm 5" H, left centre, myrtle bowl, 190mm 7½" DIA x 100mm 4", right centre, elm burr bowl, 190mm 7½" DIA x 140mm 5½" H, bottom, spalted beech bowl, 380mm 15" DIA x 75mm 3" H.

Marie to woodturning. While most girls opted for domestic science, she became the only girl in the woodwork class. Curiosity is her explanation for taking this unusual step.

Her first piece of turning was a lamp base, while a turned elephant never made it to maturity.

After leaving school, she studied for a BA (Hons) in Wood, Metal, Ceramics and Plastics at the University of Brighton, and it was while she was there that the great storm of 1987 helped push her towards woodturning.

"A friend and I went out with a trolley into the centre of Brighton to collect wood. We got a lot of elm burr and London plane and began to turn them green."

She went into business at the age of 24 with a £1,000 equipment grant and a £1,000 loan from the Prince's Youth Business Trust, opening a workshop at the Star Brewery site in Castle Ditch Lane, Lewes.

The brewery maintains that since alcohol has been responsible for inspiring much of the greatest talent mankind has had to offer, with poets, writers, painters and musicians all drawing deeply at the pump, it is fitting that an old brewery site should become a home for artists.

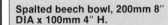

Spalted beech bowl, 200mm 8" DIA x 100mm 4" H.

Salmon gum burr bowl, 305mm 12" DIA x 100mm 4" H.

Rose-Marie had no shop to start with, selling through various retail outlets and a stall in Lewes. The shop, an extension of her workshop, was opened last year, where she sells her decorative bowls alongside hand carvings from Gambia and China.

It is called *The Space Within*, reflecting Rose-Marie's interest in Taoism. She explains:

"The Chinese philosopher Lao Tsu says the Tao is an empty vessel. It is used but never filled. I intend *The Space Within* to be a place of quiet contemplation, rather like a Japanese tea room, where people can tune in to their innermost thoughts, be at one with the beautiful objects around them and choose to have a piece they feel drawn to."

Each piece, she says, is literally a container of ▶

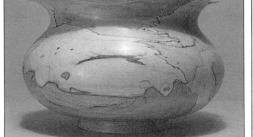

Red gum (river) bowl, 305mm 12" DIA x 4" H.

Spalted beech bowl, 230mm 9" DIA x 125mm 5" H.

Elm burr bowl, 280mm 11" DIA x 100mm 4" H.

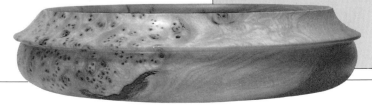

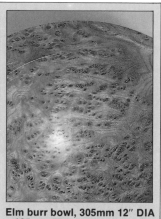

Elm burr bowl, 305mm 12″ DIA x 125mm 5″.

space, created from her inner space. And it is the space within which is the useful part of the vessel.

She wrote a dissertation on Creativity and Taoism for her degree, her interest having been aroused by a trip to China in 1979.

Taoism has influenced her work. "It's really working with nature, following the Way, or your intuition," she says. "I don't have pre-conceived ideas of what I am going to make. I put the wood on the lathe and follow the flow.

"The shapes just evolve. Sometimes it ends up totally different from how I started. You never know how it's going to turn out. Each piece of wood is different, you never get tired of exploring the grain of various woods.

"It's a bit of an adventure every time you put a piece of wood on the lathe. While you are controlling what you do, something is happening on its own as well.

"I am not meditating while I work, but it's like a form of meditation. It's an intensely satisfying experience to finish a piece you like."

Rose-Marie leaves in what others might see as imperfections, such as knots and splits, feeling they can enhance a piece if used in the right way.

"I always aim for harmony," she says. "You know when something is right. It just works. And when that happens I know I am working from my inner space."

Her decorative bowls are made from hardwoods mainly from Europe, Australia and North America. "I try to avoid rain forest timber, but it's not always easy. My supplier might tell me this wood doesn't come from there, but he's trying to make money, isn't he?"

Myrtle burr and elm burr are two of her favourite woods, but she also likes spalted beech, sycamore, hornbeam, salmon gum burr and grey gum burr.

People occasionally give her wood, sometimes asking for a bowl to be made from it, particularly if a tree in their garden has come down.

Local people and tourists are her main customers, but Rose-Marie sometimes goes to London to do a show and in 1992 exhibited at the Chelsea Crafts Fair. Her prices range from £10 to £300, and her shop is open from Tuesday to Saturday. Even men giving gratuitous advice are welcome. ■

Elm burr bowl, 305mm 12″ DIA x 100mm 4″ H.

Mali root bowl, 255mm 10″ DIA x 50mm 2″ H.

Sanding a bowl on the lathe.

Elm burr bowl, 460mm 18″ DIA x 100mm 4″ H.

Jarrah burr bowl, 200mm 8″ DIA x 100mm 4″ H.

DELVIN' WITH MELVYN

REG SHERWIN

Melvyn Firmager is one of that rare species of Brits, a pioneering woodturner. Reg Sherwin reports on a hollow form course with the master at his Somerset farmhouse.

Melvyn Firmager is one of a rare breed — a pioneering woodturner. "That's not so rare", I hear you cry. "Pioneering turners have been around for years. Look at Prestini, Ellsworth, Hogbin, Stubbs, Lindquist, Moulthrop, all pioneers, and by no means the only ones."

But Melvyn Firmager is British. It's this which puts him firmly on the rare breeds list. He's not the only 'Brit' on the list, but there aren't nearly as many British pioneers as there are American.

Melvyn started turning round about 1980, took the great step into professional turning six years later, and set out on big adventures into hollow form turning two years after that.

Having decided to concentrate on the hollow closed form, the technique of hollowing out thin-walled vessels through small openings, Melvyn found the tools available at that time limited his technical boundaries.

He spent time watching David Ellsworth demonstrate his well established methods of producing hollow closed forms, at the 1987 Loughborough Seminar.

David had generously been open about the development of the specialist tools he uses to achieve the incredible results which have made his name part of modern woodturning's language.

Melvyn was inspired by this first meeting with David, but was unwilling to follow exactly the path of the master. He wanted to explore a different route. So he set out to develop tools to suit his particular situation.

Initially, these tools were little more than unorthodox grinding angles and profiles on the existing and easily available deep-fluted bowl gouges.

These new profiles demanded new techniques as well. Indeed, the two learning areas went hand in hand. It would be more accurate to say each new development in one area demanded more exploration into the other.

Some successes followed, and inevitably some failures, the latter chiefly being due to not having the tools for the job. So, proving that necessity really is the mother of invention, Melvyn set about designing some.

Incidentally, the refined versions of these special tools, shown in Photo 1, are now available from Melvyn on mail order.

I'd known most of this through talking to other turners before I met Melvyn. I'd spoken to him briefly back in '89 at one of Del Stubbs' last UK demonstrations, but my first real conversation with Melvyn came later.

It was one of those conversations which could easily have taken us not into friendship but

Photo 1 Special tools and standard tools with special grinds.

> '**We all had problems with stance, something I am embarrassed to admit after 25 years of turning.**'

animosity. Happily, we both rose above the situation, agreed to differ and became firm friends.

So much so that when Nick Hough took over the editorship of this magazine he agreed to my suggestion that I do a two-day course with Melvyn and then write it up from the practical turner's point of view.

Melvyn runs three types of course — *Beginner and Beyond*, *Wet Turned Natural Edge*, and *Advanced Hollow Form*.

I decided on the latter course for several reasons, one being I had no 'hands-on' experience of the type of small hole excavating which would be the culmination of such a course.

Another reason for the choice was the course ▶

dates were the only ones available in our full programmes of teaching and demonstrations.

In fact, Melvyn was just five days away from his first demonstration trip to the USA, and by the time this article is published, will have completed his second trip.

With four purpose-built lathes and a standard spindle turning lathe in his Somerset workshop, Melvyn is able to take four students at a time.

The workshop is one of a number of buildings in the yard of Nut Tree Farm, where Melvyn, his wife Anne and their two children Cori and Raz live. Photo 2 shows Raz turning on 'his' lathe, under the watchful eye of Dad.

Photo 2 Small hollow form turner in the making.

Photo 3 Melvyn, Walter and Volkmar getting stuck in!

Photo 4 Horizontal hand support — position of fingers and thumb.

Photo 5 Horizontal hand support — the actual grip.

My fellow course students were to be Volkmar Zimmer from Germany and Walter Decruy from Belgium. I had met both of them previously at one of the earlier AWGB Loughborough seminars. I remembered Volkmar particularly, as his was the first stone-embedded turning I had seen.

I'd driven down to Somerset on the first morning of the course but Volkmar, Walter and their wives had arrived the day before and were using the bed and breakfast facility run by Anne.

Melvyn's teaching method, at least to start with, was to explain what would be done, to demonstrate it and then watch us work.

Individual problems were dealt with immediately, while common ones were looked at, discussed and rectified collectively.

We all had problems with stance, something I am embarrassed to admit after 25 years of turning. But I have to acknowledge that once I allowed my shoulders to fall, and the neck muscles to relax, I was far more comfortable.

I am not going to get too involved with the technical aspects of the course here, for a number of reasons. The main one is that I have a lot to learn about what is to me a whole new ball game, and so I am not the person to explain new techniques. As with most new situations, the basics, once explained, need a lot of initially supervised practice.

Melvyn showed us these basics, took us through the problems all newcomers encounter, patiently guided us back onto the path from which we strayed, with alarming regularity in my case, and frequently pulled us out of the pitfalls down which he had himself plunged in his own early explorations.

Photo 3 shows Melvyn, Walter and Volkmar

sometimes leads to road safety problems, when passing cyclists glance into the yard to see a sandalled, bewhiskered and unruly-haired gentleman adopting the crouching position.

He is bending forward at the waist, hands on his knees and a face screwed up in concentration. He is either squinting or has one eye closed, with one ear pointing to the sky and the other towards the ground.

The woodturners among us will realise Melvyn is studying the form of his latest creation which is out of sight of the road and still in the horizontal position on the lathe.

But more than one poor, unenlightened, and by now alarmed, cyclist has been known to wobble uncontrollably into an adjacent ditch.

Inspiration comes to Melvyn from many sources, notably Ellsworth, Nish, Stubbs and recently, Hosaluk, to name but a few.

It also comes from nature. Photo 6 is just such ▶

> **'This sometimes leads to road safety problems, when passing cyclists glance into the yard to see a sandalled, bewhiskered and unruly-haired gentleman adopting the crouching position.'**

discussing the use of superglue, often needed to repair unexpected problems caused by wet timber movement, a moment's inattention with a tool, or some other unplanned contingency.

Photos 4 and 5 show just one of Melvyn's innovations. The toolrest is drilled and threaded to take a suitably sized metal rod.

This in turn gives the front hand extra purchase on the rest without inhibiting the movement of the tool along or over the rest during the cuts. Photo 4 shows the position of fingers and thumb and Photo 5 the actual 'grip'.

A feature of Melvyn's hollow form lathes is that each of them has an arrangement where the power can be switched on or off with the foot.

This important safety feature allows for careful insertion of the chosen turning tool through the narrow entry hole while the lathe is stationary.

It also allows the lathe to be switched off with a foot should a situation arise where the hands are otherwise engaged. This is particularly important on some of his larger work, where safety and stability during manufacture is vital.

The tallest closed form Melvyn has turned to date was 660mm 26" high x 355mm 14" DIA, and the widest piece 710mm 28" DIA x 570mm 20" tall.

The workshop Melvyn uses has a concrete floor raised from the ground level of the yard. This

Photo 6 You work it out!

Photo 7 Part of the gallery . . .

Photo 8 . . . tends to spill out into other areas.

an example. How many of us would have cut the branch off the main section of the 'blank', if indeed we had bothered to rescue it from the log basket in the first place? The finished piece on the left gives a clue to the probable final shape of the blank.

Photo 7 shows some of the pieces Melvyn has in his gallery which also serves as an entrance hall. To add variation, the work of other crafts people is also on show, but as you might expect, the woodturning stands out.

The 'gallery' also spreads into the Firmager living room, (Photo 8) where new work jostles with early pieces, easy chairs and Bed and Breakfast visitors.

Photo 9 shows an assortment of finished

Photo 9 The seasoning shelf.

pieces, some of which still have some movement left in them, not yet having settled down to the new life Melvyn has breathed into them.

The laburnum piece to the right of the front row is some 150mm 6" tall and now has pride of place in my own humble collection of other turners' work.

The globe pictured seems to be fighting a losing battle against the ever encroaching sculptural turnings which have made their creator world famous.

For further details of Melvyn's courses, demonstrations or specialist tools, send a SAE 215mm 8½" x 115mm 4½" to him at Nut Tree Farm, Stoughton Cross, Wedmore, Somerset BS28 4QP. Tel/Fax: Wedmore 0934 712404. ■

DISH TO FISH

VIC WOOD

Our Australian adviser shows how a disaster can become inspiration for a new work.

Robert Mortimer was an apprentice pattern maker in the 1970s when he learned about faceplates and split turnings. He began commercial woodturning in the early 80s and now operates in all forms of woodwork.

Robert is environment-conscious and his timber comes from the forest floor, local tips, garden tree loppers and the remnants of bush fires, as well as from commercial suppliers.

He does what he enjoys most, earning a living from fine woodwork with his family of Wadkin machines, which have enabled his business to be versatile.

Robert's business is called Cooinda Woodcrafts. Cooinda is Aboriginal for Happy House, and this is the atmosphere that greets you in his workshop.

Robert Mortimer, 4930 Great Eastern Highway, Mahogany Creek, Western Australia 6072.

What do you do if the project you started out with turns out wrong, through a fault in the wood?

Well, with a bit of imagination, the disaster can be turned to advantage, and another completely different work can be salvaged from the wreckage.

This is what happened to woodturner/carver Robert Mortimer, who lives in the appropriately named town of Mahogany Creek, Western Australia.

Robert set out to turn a vase from an interesting piece of camphor laurel. The vase turned out well (Photo 1).

Unfortunately there was dry rot in a section near the stem which caused the piece to break (Photo 2).

Using his pattern making skills, Robert reshaped the top section of the broken piece and carved it to make a fish's head sculpture. ■

Photo 1 The original vase.

Photo 2 Dry rot caused the break . . .

Photo 3 . . . So it became a fish sculpture instead.

A MEETING WIT

MERRYLL SAYLAN

Merryll first met the "grand old man of woodturning" 20 years ago when, as a student, she visited his workshop to learn from the master. Now she has re-visited him to discover more about the craftsman and his work.

Merryll Saylan started turning in 1974. Having graduated from UCLA the previous year she enrolled in the woodworking programme and turning was a requirement.

Her art school background has much to do with her feeling for colours and textures which are a distinctive feature of her work.

Merryll is well known in the UK as a result of a 12-month residency at the Grizedale Forestry Centre in the Lake District in 1990/91, and her demonstrations at national woodworking shows and exhibitions, including the Loughborough '91 international seminar.

She has become a regular visitor to the UK, and contributor to *Woodturning*.

When I was a student in art school some 20 years ago, in a woodworking programme, woodturning was one of the things required of us. Bob Stocksdale's name kept coming up and his bowls set the standard.

Students tried to achieve the beautiful forms he made, tried turning bowls as thin, utilising the beautiful and exotic woods he was known for. We discussed his work as we did other craftsmen.

A romantic story circulated about how he had learned to turn while being in a Conscientious Objectors' camp during World War II. Several friends I knew had been in the Japanese internment camps during the war and I assumed Bob had been at a similar place and whiled away his time by turning. I was wrong.

During those student years there were two exhibitions in Southern California, where I was living, which we students greatly looked forward to. One of them, California Design, was particularly exciting because it not only displayed the most contemporary craft work being done, but also the best and newest of industrial design. You could see Charles Eames' newest chairs, furniture by Sam Maloof, and bowls by Bob Stocksdale.

The other exhibition was held at the annual Los Angeles County Fair. It was just like a country fair with champion animals, plants and produce, and crafts. The crafts just happened to be by people like Stocksdale. Living spaces would be set up, furnished by craftsmen.

During the 1950s, Bob visited the fair, overheard a conversation about "shoemaker's

Bob Stocksdale demonstrating at a Woodturning Conference several years ago at the California College of Art, Oakland, California. Photo: Ed Saylan.

Bob Stocksdale. Photo: Ed Saylan.

'I'm the only craftsman I know of who has always maintained regular hours right from the start. I never worked more than a 40-hour week.'

H BOB STOCKSDALE

children", turned around and said, "You must be Sam Maloof". They've been friends ever since. Bob still supplies Maloof with wood plugs for his furniture. Bob demonstrated at this fair once, but it ran for 17 days and was a bit too much.

My woodworking class visited artists in their studios, and we travelled up north to visit Stocksdale. I was thrilled. It seems rather silly, but one of the things I remember so clearly from that visit was a technique I still use: a method of mixing different sawdusts from a variety of woods with glue to fill checks. You could match any colour of timber mixing and matching the dusts. The other major impression I came away with was Bob's love of wood — there were pieces and logs of it all around.

Now that I live in the same community, this was a delightful opportunity to interview Bob and get to know him better. I particularly wanted to learn about his early years, how he really started turning, and to clarify some of the stories I'd heard.

Bob grew up on a farm but always had an interest in woodworking from early boyhood. He got his first cheap lathe when he was about 15. It was powered by a petrol engine as the farm had no electricity. He couldn't turn bowls on it — the shaft had no thread and he had no faceplate.

He had a small workshop and was doing reproduction and refinishing, restoration and repairs, and sometimes needed to make a spindle or a table leg.

Below and right, **lignum vitae bowl** (Nicaragua) 150mm 6" H x 190mm 7½" DIA.

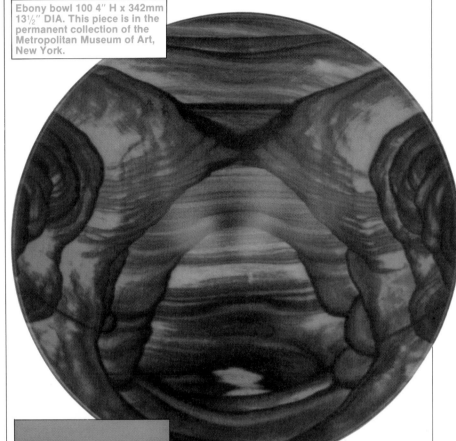

Ebony bowl 100 4" H x 342mm 13½" DIA. This piece is in the permanent collection of the Metropolitan Museum of Art, New York.

Bob later worked in two factories where he learned to use all kinds of woodworking machinery. One factory made cedar chests, and the other cracker peels — large balsa and plywood paddles, about 2' wide and 4' long, for picking up crackers, or biscuits, as they came out of the oven.

They required, surprisingly, a complicated lot of woodworking skills and tools. Bob made them from start to finish and learned to use all the different machines. When he was drafted and mentioned this past experience, he naturally got put in charge of the woodshop.

Bob was a Conscientious Objector during the war, as were his mother, older and younger brother. His father and youngest brother were not. His older brother, as a farmer, did not have to serve. Bob's service as a CO was for the Forest Service, at the headquarters in Michigan. The CO's job was to replant pine trees that had been cut down in the 1800s rebuilding Chicago after the fire.

Bob also worked in the woodshop making whatever was needed, such as tool boxes, tool▶

sheds, signs, and once a 'two-hole' toilet. The CO's were later transferred west to help fight forest fires. They received no pay for their work, and Bob even contributed to his own upkeep, out of his savings, until his funds ran out. He served a total of three years and ten months.

One day, a Forest Service man suggested turning a bowl on a lathe, a Delta 12″. They hunted up some cherry and walnut chunks and made several bowls.

''My first customer was a Quaker woman from Columbus, Ohio, who visited the camp,'' he recalled. ''She told me she liked what I was doing and said she'd take most anything I wanted to make, but 'whatever you do, keep up the quality. I don't care what it costs — what I want is quality.' That was in 1944, and she was in business way before I met her. And I had a show there two years ago.''

When the men fought fires, sometimes they worked for a week, day and night. A work day was counted as 8 hours, so a 24-hour fire day constituted three working days, and Bob started accumulating long furloughs. He came down on visits to the San Francisco area where he picked up some work doing furniture repairs, turning , and making replacement parts.

The owner of the Hudson Furniture Store would save up work for him for the times he was able to come down. He had his own tools shipped out to the camp where he set up and ran a woodshop for the other CO's to use, making whatever they needed. He brought wood back for them when he was in the Bay Area and began making his contacts with wood dealers.

When released, he and two friends decided to settle in Berkeley. Since none of them had any money, Bob offered to help buy a house if it had room for a woodshop. They bought a duplex that Bob still lives in today. His friends, who were married, each took one side of the house, and Bob took a back bedroom.

He immediately excavated 18″ in the basement, put in a concrete floor and is still working in that same space. He bought a lathe, spindle shaper and bandsaw for $100. Eventually he bought the house from his friends as they got work elsewhere and moved on.

The house is a modest, typical Berkeley wood clad cottage, but upon entering the space opens up to high ceilings and skylights. There is an open loft where Bob's wife, Kay Sekimachi, a well-known craftswoman, does weaving. The floors are made of teak that Bob himself laid. His bowls and platters sit atop the hood over the stove drying, and a walnut dining table and chairs of Sam Maloof's greet you. The house is filled with furniture and pieces of Bob's and Kay's and their friends. It is warm and comfortable and fits the two perfectly.

Bob loves to talk about wood. He told me about a hardwood place he dealt with in those days and

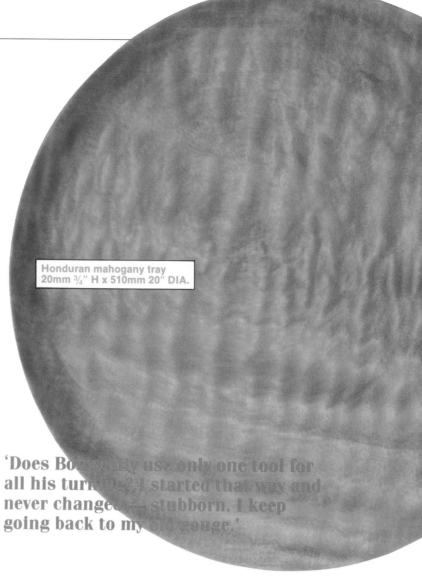

Honduran mahogany tray
20mm ¾″ H x 510mm 20″ DIA.

'Does Bob really use only one tool for all his turning? I started that way and never changed — stubborn. I keep going back to my old gouge.'

how he got hold of some wood pulled out of the Fairmount Hotel after the big fire. The carpenters wouldn't use it because it made them sneeze. It was jenisero from Guatemala, also called guanacaste, and how he still has a few pieces of it left.

He tells me about the macadamia he got in Hawaii, and how he brought back a piece of wood called Pride of India. ''Did you ever hear of that wood? Mark Twain mentions it in his book *Letters from Hawaii* because of its beautiful flower, though the wood isn't that much.''

Bob's first wife had a teaching job in England. He came along and spent the year travelling all over the country. I forgot to ask what wood he brought back from that trip.

He started turning bowls as soon as he was released. ''During my time in the camps I established connections with lumber companies not only here but in Los Angeles. I had good sources of supply for imported woods as well as local woods. That was a big help, to know where to get it.'' There were not a lot of craftspeople at the time — the early 1950s — and through Gump's in San Francisco, he established other places to sell his work such as George Jensen's in New York.

Snakewood bowl (Suriname)
75mm 3″ H x 180mm 7″ DIA.

Masur birch bowl (Russia)
100mm 4″ H x 115mm 4½″ DIA.

Pistachio bowl 100mm 4″ H x 190mm 7½″ DIA.

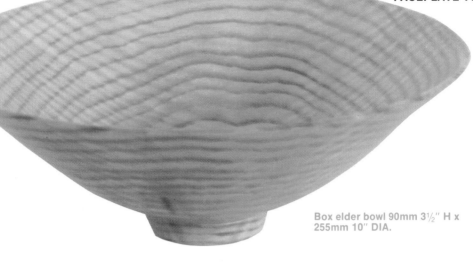

Box elder bowl 90mm 3½" H x 255mm 10" DIA.

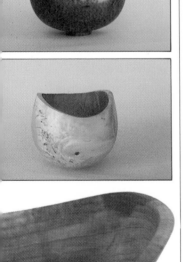

I asked Bob if he had much contact with other woodturners in those early days. He replied no — there weren't any! What about James Prestini?

"I visited him in Chicago when he still doing turning. He worked in a corner of a furniture factory and would get wood from them and have the factory throw the finish on. He was a full time teacher, taught at the Chicago Art Institute."

In those days Bob was a member of a craft guild, the Designer/Craftsmen of California, a cross-media group. They had a retail shop out in the Cliff House in San Francisco.

I had to ask Bob whether the stories of him using only one tool for all his turning were true.

"I started that way and never changed — stubborn. Jerry Glaser keeps sending me these new gouges that he makes. I try them, and keep going back to my old gouge. Maybe he'll wean me away."

Then there were the tales about 36 grit sandpaper. ("That Bob Stocksdale — he doesn't turn, he uses 36 grit sandpaper!")

Bob laughed and commented: "I have 36 grit. I've used it. It depends on the wood, you know, and that lignum vitae, I start with 36 grit on that because it's so difficult to cut it. With sandpaper, 36 grit takes it off real neat. So I use it on that. Any extremely hard wood sometimes, like that African blackwood, I use it sometimes on the inside of the bowl. Most turning I start with 50 grit.

"You can scrape it down with real sharp tools, razor sharp, but you can knock it off three or four times as fast with sandpaper. Shaping is better, the rotary disk works better on the outside of the bowl."

I next asked Bob if he had ever taught or taken in students. He replied no, he had just done some demonstrating. "I don't like to teach," he said. "I'm allergic to teaching." But he doesn't mind when people visit him at work — he says it gives him a chance to rest a little.

Bob has been referred to as the "grand old man of woodturning", and at 79 it's probably true. He attributes his longevity at his work to his regular working hours.

"I'm the only craftsman I know of who has always maintained regular hours from the beginning," he said. "I never worked more than a 40-hour week, for as long as I've been turning bowls, never worked weekends, nights or anything like that. If I had worn myself out, you know, grinding out bowls, night and day and all that stuff it would have gotten to be such a drudgery."

He's now cut his week down to 20 hours and says he's making more money than ever. I wanted to know if Bob's prices had changed suddenly with the growth and interest in woodturning, but Bob said no, it had been a steady growth.

He told me sometimes he had a piece he was particularly fond of and he would put the price up and it seemed to sell quicker than the ones with lower prices. Certainly, the list of collectors and museums such as the Metropolitan Museum of Art in New York, The Boston Museum of Art, the Smithsonian Institution, that have his work is quite long and impressive.

As an art student, innovation, doing new work, was one of the most important things. At school , we discussed artists like Maloof and Stocksdale and the kind of work they did and the length of time they had been doing it.

I asked Bob about his shapes and forms and whether he started out with them. He told me his forms kept getting more refined and with more variations. He preferred doing decorative bowls over salad bowls, though he felt he could sell every salad bowl he made. The decorative bowls were more challenging, and the wood he got was frequently too small for salad bowls. That was another story oft told — how people gave Bob wood, all kinds because of his love of it.

One of the primary goals in Bob's work has been to uncover the unusual colour and grain in wood. And, he's been doing it for all these years.

I feel a debt not only to the beautiful forms that Bob Stocksdale makes and that inspired me in my work, but to the philosophy, honesty in his work, and consistency of how he has lived his life. This particular strength of character is what makes his work beautiful, alive, and enduring. ■

Mosaic magic

This thin-walled bowl with dancing girl motif may not be for beginners, but Geoff O'Loughlin shows what wonders can be achieved by those turners prepared to go to any lengths to achieve an artistic effect.

Translucent colours have appealed to me since I was a child, gazing at the stained glass windows in church while my grandfather preached. I now make a colourful thin-walled bowl equivalent, using tinted epoxy resin with wood.

My method also offers scope for creative design or mosaic work, and the incorporation of other materials, if desired. The size of the bowl is limited only by the centre height of the lathe.

A bowl of this type (Photos 1 to 3), which was shown at the Melbourne Working With Wood Show last year,
prompted a number of visitors to ask how it was made and how long it took me. I thought fellow woodturners might also be interested.

The bowl was made over a period of four weeks, but much of this time was spent waiting for the epoxy resin to cure properly. I kept no record of the actual time taken, but it was much less than it would have been had the pieces been glued together individually, as some had imagined.

'Sacrificial' bowl

I turned a `sacrificial' bowl of medium density fibre board (MDF), but only finished the inside properly. This was to provide support for the pieces of wood and coloured resin during assembly, and was eventually turned away completely.

To obtain a hemispherical surface, I used a tool with an adjustable tip. It was held by a bolt screwed into a threaded hole at the edge of a faceplate mounted horizontally in the toolrest base (Photos 4 and 5).

The bolt was tightened sufficiently
to hold the tool firmly while allowing it to swing sideways. A lock nut on the bolt held it in place.

After turning the interior, a final smoothing cut was made with the cutting tip advanced a fraction. It's important to keep the pivotal point in line with the lathe centre to produce a spherical surface shape.

One coat of sanding sealer was applied to the inside and a red gum ring 8mm ⁵⁄₁₆" thick was glued to the top and turned to form a lip (FIG 1). The MDF bowl pictured is an earlier model, and has a narrow edge.

Mosaic wall

To assemble the mosaic wall of the bowl, I cut pieces of New Guinea walnut and arranged them as shown in

Photo 4 The scraper in position for finishing the bowl interior.

Photo 5 The HSS adjustable tip.

Photo 6 MDF pieces show how the walnut ones were assembled.

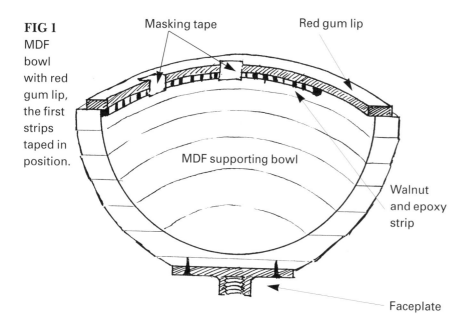

FIG 1 MDF bowl with red gum lip, the first strips taped in position.

Masking tape

Red gum lip

MDF supporting bowl

Walnut and epoxy strip

Faceplate

Photo 6 using sections of MDF. The pieces, which varied in thickness, were separated by thin slats of wood, in this case dental tongue depressors.

MDF pieces were then glued to the bottom and sides of the pack and the slats removed, after which clear epoxy casting resin, tinted with artist's oil, was poured into the gaps.

I used ultramarine, cobalt violet and viridian in very small amounts. Transparent dyes may also be available from epoxy resin suppliers.

When mixing the two resin components, it's wise to stir slowly, to avoid bubbles. At least three days were needed to cure the resin sufficiently, otherwise it chipped easily.

When cured, the block was sawn across the grain into 3mm ⅛" thick slabs, which were then cut into 5mm ³⁄₁₆" wide strips, as in Photo 7.

I've found that by lying a strip along a radiator the resin becomes flexible and will retain its shape when cool, as shown by the bent strip in Photo 7.

Contours

This is fortunate, as it allows the strips to conform exactly to the MDF bowl contours before gluing them together. The first piece was taken off the radiator and held against the red gum rim with a piece of masking tape.

I repeated this until the top layer was complete (FIG 1). Then the others were arranged in the same way. After completion, all pieces were removed, the layers being kept separate from each other.

Each layer was then glued into position using epoxy glue, with enough black pigment to make it opaque. To apply the glue, it was first spread on to glass with a palette knife. Then the top edge and ends of each strip were pressed onto it before being pushed into position.

Each piece can be taped in position, but I got my wife – wearing rubber gloves – to keep the pieces in position until the final segment of each ring was placed. Each layer was then self-supporting.

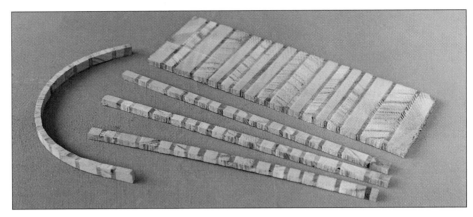

Photo 7 The block is sawn into slabs and then into strips. One strip remains bent after heating

I drew the dancing girls on the end grain of mahogany blocks, then cut them out roughly on a bandsaw (Photo 8). Each block provided four figures, when sawn transversely.

The underside of each figure was sanded to the correct profile by holding it against a sanding disc hollowed out to the same curvature as the bowl, and having four pieces of 120 grit

Photo 8 Figures are rough shaped with the bandsaw

▶

FIG 2 Dremel tool set up with drill bits for smoothing the edge of the figures.

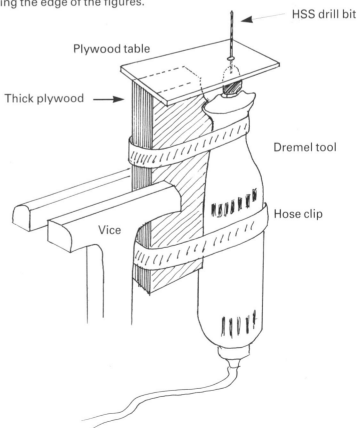

HSS drill bit

Plywood table

Thick plywood

Dremel tool

Hose clip

Vice

'I kept no record of the actual time taken (to make the bowl) but it was much less than it would have been had the pieces been glued together individually, as some had imagined'.

Photo 2 The dancing girl motif in the base of the bowl

Photo 1 A thin walled bowl with dancing girls

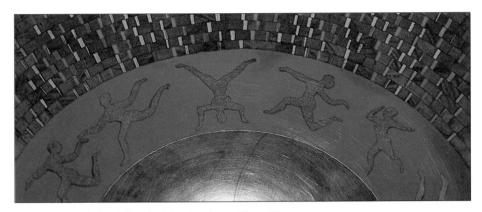

Photo 3 Highlighted detail of the dancing girl motif.

Photo 9 A hollow MDF sanding disc for shaping the back of the figures

The author

Geoff O'Loughlin's former work as a research scientist involved the use of epoxy resin, in which insects and plants had to be embedded for sectioning before they could be viewed under the microscope. It gave him an appreciation of the properties of this resin and, since his retirement 11 years ago, has led him to explore ways of incorporating it into ornamental woodturning. Also a painter, Geoff shows his work in the galleries of three Australian states. He feels membership of the 150-strong Peninsula Woodturners' Guild in Melbourne has helped him solve many problems and has added to the enjoyment of his turning.

His hobbies are collecting antique lathes, brass microscopes, and keyboard instruments.

He lives in Beaumaris, Victoria, Australia.

paper stapled to the MDF disc (Photo 9)

I smoothed the edges of the figures with the side of a metal drill bit mounted in a Dremel tool (FIG 2), then glued them into position.

The quantity of epoxy resin needed to fill the space between the figures was calculated and then poured into the bottom of the MDF bowl.

I loosely covered the resin with two thicknesses of thin polythene film, then tipped sand onto the polythene to force the resin up among the figures.

After allowing three days for the resin to cure I turned the bowl's interior using the same tool as before, and sanded with 320 and 600 grit paper.

▶

As the bowl would be thin and might have needed support while I turned the outside, I turned a solid MDF plug to roughly fit the inside. The interior surface was covered with strips of packaging tape for protection, and this was smeared with petroleum jelly to act as a separator.

I covered the plug with a layer of newly mixed plaster to provide firm contact, and pushed into the bowl by winding in the tailstock live centre (FIG 3).

After the plaster had set, the 'sacrificial' supporting bowl was sacrificed by carefully turning it away to expose the bowl's outside surface.

The only tool used here was a scraper consisting of a tungsten tooth from a circular saw, silver soldered to a narrow steel rod. I particularly like this scraper, which also makes a nice parting tool, but I suppose any small scraper would have done.

I still feel safer with scrapers in high risk situations, and they work well with epoxy resin, producing long ribbons.

The plug was removed, the bowl shell (now 2mm ³⁄₃₂" thick) separated, and the packaging tape removed. At this stage the bowl consisted of a 360mm 14 ¼" DIA shell with a 140mm 5 ½" DIA hole in the bottom.

The bowl base

The base was turned from a block of four red gum lengths of square sec-tion glued together, the grain running vertically.

The base's upper surface was turned with the pivoted tool as before to obtain the same curvature. The top edge was turned to a thickness like that of the bowl shell, and the diameter carefully reduced until a good fit was obtained.

I glued the base into position using epoxy glue, holding it with masking tape until the glue had set.

The matched pieces were trimmed on the lathe, the inside while the base was held in a four-jaw chuck, and the outside by having the rim in a jam chuck, held in place by a rubber tip on the tailstock live centre. The bowl was finished with Danish oil. ■

FIG 3 Supporting the bowl for removal of the MDF bowl and for finishing the outer surface.

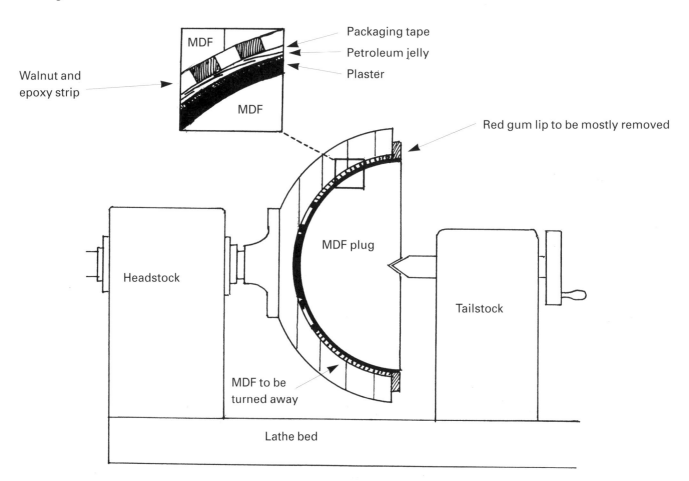

Matt Calder, 28, has been turning for nine years and became a full-time turner six years ago.

After a brief spell at art college he served an apprenticeship as a furniture maker and restorer. Three years later he spent some time at the Hooke Park Forestry Project in Dorset where he gained valuable experience in forestry work and chainsaw skills.

In the adjacent Parnham workshops he had a few lessons with the resident turner Cecil Jordan who told him he would never make a turner!

His first woodturning workshop was near a potter in Somerset and he drew much inspiration from the potter's forms.

He has since staged four solo exhibitions as well as joint shows, and for the last four years has been craftsman in residence at the National Trust's Buckland Abbey at Yelverton, Devon, where he has his workshop and gallery.

The bulk of his work is done on a home-made A-frame lathe of welded angle iron with a 2½" HP motor and swing of 1220mm 48". It has a 16-speed gear arrangement allowing speeds down to 50 RPM.

Matt likes working with burrs, and favourite timbers include sycamore and holly. He looks to the earth and environmental imagery for inspiration and is currently exploring multi-axis techniques and willow weaving.

MATT CALDER

A basketwork top can give an unusual look and feel to a bowl. Matt, who specialises in the technique, shows how it's done.

One of the advantages of being in a combined work space with other makers is the crossover of ideas and techniques. A well-known basketmaker occupies a workshop next to mine and, being always on the lookout for new ideas, I thought it would be a challenge to incorporate some weaving into my work.

I had used willow before on a few pieces, but the outcome had always looked a little 'bitty' and unfinished. Most of my work is not necessarily planned — I try to rely on a crossover between myself and the material during the making process to dictate the final outcome.

For me, however, weaving willow is not so spontaneous, so the whole piece had to be sketched and drawn from the start.

I had already decided that I wanted handles on this particular piece, so with this in mind the 760mm 30" x 180mm 7"

GET WEAVING ON YOUR BOWLS

Photo 14 The finished piece.

Photo 2 Cutting the back of the blank. Note the shallow bevel.

yew blank was roughly shaped with a chainsaw and mounted on the lathe with a 100mm 4" faceplate and 6 x 38mm 1½" coach bolts (Photo 1).

With two such aggressive chunks of timber sticking out from the sides, it's common sense to take it easy in the initial roughing out. However, green yew is very fibrous and strong, so I could move on from the standard 12mm ½" HSS bowl gouge to a 20mm ¾" bowl gouge, very quickly.

The initial lathe speed was about 60 RPM, which I could increase to about 120 RPM once the blank was balanced.

This is where I prefer an A-frame design lathe to the more standard box style machine, as it's possible to get right behind the work. From a safety point of view if nothing else, this is a real advantage (Photo 2).

Once the underside was shaped, leaving a 25mm 1" foot of waste to remove the screw holes later, and the position of the handles was finalised, I used an Arbortech on a vari-speed 115mm 4½" angle grinder to remove the waste around the handles and roughly trim to size (Photos 3 and 4).

Getting the length of the handles right was important at this stage — I wanted the blank to feel comfortable before continuing. The handle length felt best at about half the diameter of the bowl area. Any longer and they seemed cumbersome, any shorter and I guessed they would have looked dumpy (Photo 5).

Removing the bowl area was relatively straightforward. The lathe ran smoothly at around 700 RPM, and I could remove the wet timber quickly with a 20mm ¾" gouge (Photo 6).

I like my gouges ground at almost right angles, so the tool handle is almost horizontal. It's a little difficult to get a good edge, but I find it a comfortable angle to work at.

The mouth of the bowl had to be fairly wide to take the willow

Photo 1 Mounting the blank on the lathe.

Photo 3 Cleaning up the front of the blank.

> **'Most of my work is not necessarily planned — I try to rely on a crossover between myself and the material.'**

uprights, so accepting that it was going to be a heavyish piece (give me substance over feather-weight any day), I left a good 20mm ¾" wall to the bowl.

Yew is one of the most stable woods I have worked with — as long as the drying process is not too rapid there is very little mishaping or degrade, so I was confident that I could finish the weave and let the piece dry afterwards without any distortion occurring.

I used my blowtorch to dry the surface of the bowl area prior to sanding (Photo 7). This is an effective way of getting an idea of the final figure.

At this stage I selected the 1525mm 60" willow rods and drilled 10mm ⅜" holes to accept the butt ends. After the holes were drilled the bowl area was dried again with the torch and sanded up to 240 grit (Photo 8). ▶

Photo 6 Removing the waste from the bowl area.

Photo 7 Drying the surface with a blowtorch prior to sanding.

Photo 4 Removing the waste with the Arbortech.

Photo 5 The handles trimmed to size.

Photo 8 Power sanding with a 125mm 5" pad.

Photo 9 Pushing the rods into place.

Photo 10 Keeping the rods moist with a garden sprayer.

Photo 12 Two thirds of the way through the weave.

Photo 11 A tentative start on the weaving — note reference book close at hand.

The willow I used was a locally grown stripped white and had to be soaked for about half an hour to make it pliable enough to bend at right angles without kinking.

The rods were then pushed into place (Photo 9). Any that I felt could have been a bit loose, I secured with a dab of Zap glue.

At this point I should point out that as this was only my third or fourth attempt at a weave this complicated, I am in no position to write with any authority about the technique of weaving, I have listed a few easily obtainable books at the end of this article, all of which cover the subject in far more detail than I have space for here.

However, I will stress a few important points. It is necessary to keep the willow wet during the process — a garden sprayer is excellent for the job (Photo 10). You must also keep the right gap between the rods — too far apart and the weave is loose and slack, too close and it's a real hassle getting around the tight bends, especially towards the end.

Photos 11 and 12 show the weaving in progress — plenty of space is needed for this part of the operation. Photo 13 shows the weave completed, but still with plenty of hand sanding to get through.

The garden sprayer leaves the piece pretty soaked, so it's important to dry it out as thoroughly as possible before final sanding. I left it for about three months at normal temperature before sanding to 360 grit. Photo 14 shows the finished piece.

Other willow projects have included whole fill-in areas, to create a complete globe (Photo 15). The natural gaps between the weave show glimpses of the interior (sometimes brightly coloured) but also give the idea of a solid, impenetrable object.

I'm quite prepared to accept that my methods of production are technically lacking, but whatever challenges I present myself with, my concern is with the final outcome — the object that will prevail.

My line up of tools is purposely basic and it's this simplicity that I try to reflect in my work. ■

> **'Whatever challenges I present myself with, my concern is with the final outcome — the object that will prevail.'**

Photo 15 Yew globe 460mm 18" DIA with weave fill-in to create a mixture of textures.

Photo 13 The completed weave, prior to hand sanding.

TECHNICAL

T Doing what

If a piece of wood has an interesting grain pattern, a quirky fault, a strange shape or evidence of some interesting past, why not make use of these features, provided design is not ignored?

The rapid growth of interest in bowl turning over the past decade has led to a lot being written about vessel design, the writers often emphasising the importance of getting the basics right and not being fooled by fancy wood grain into forgetting line, form and proportion.

For example, in *Turned Bowl Design,* Richard Raffan says, "It is easy to produce a bowl that, by virtue of its rich colour and/or wild grain patterns will draw gasps of admiration".

He goes on to write of turners showing "... every split, hole and defect imaginable, located without apparent heed to the most elementary aesthetic or practical considerations.

"It often reflects", he adds, "a willingness to rely on quality of wood to carry a poorly designed or badly executed piece of work".

You only have to skim through previous issues of *Woodturning* to find general agreement. What constitutes good design may sometimes be disputed, but the principle is good and I for one would not disagree.

It's interesting, therefore, to see how often even very good turners rely on wood features to make their work more attractive and, if they are professional, to help it sell.

Perhaps the principle needs to be modified to something like: "Given that the design is equally good, a piece with interesting wood features will usually sell before one that is made from bland timber".

RAW MATERIALS

This may be stating the obvious, but it doesn't hurt to keep it in mind when searching out raw materials.

Like Richard Raffan, I cringe when I hear turners talk of "revealing that which is in the wood", as if there is some mystical process at work.

But if a piece of wood has an interesting grain pattern, a quirky fault, a strange shape or evidence of some interesting past — why not use it?

Trees are great recording instruments. Almost everything that has happened to a tree will be faithfully preserved by it. It may be a particularly dry or wet period in its life.

A fire may leave scars which have been overgrown by new wood. A branch which has snapped off may be overgrown but remain as an interesting inclusion, or it may allow invasion by rot, insects or some other natural phenomenon to change the structure of the tree.

I have found bottles, horseshoes and innumerable lengths of wire embedded deep in the heartwood of trees, often with unfortunate results for my chainsaw or gouge.

Even after a tree has been cut down, it can continue to be interestingly modified. A fence post may be drilled for wire, allowing fungus invasions, or it may grow a beautiful coat of moss on one side.

It's interesting to turn a 100-year-old fence post, leave the moss on and then say, "This side faced such-and-such a way for over 100 years".

I suggest we can have the best of both worlds if we observe two basic principles:
● **Design must not be sacrificed to wood features.**
● **Interesting wood features should not be ignored because of wrong adherence to design theory.**

There are times when I turn wood without regard to grain and colour. It may be because I want to do a simple shape that speaks for itself, or I am going to blowtorch, stain, paint, texture, or otherwise traumatise it, and in the process obscure the grain or features.

Photo 1 shows an example of where the grain is secondary to the form and other work. It could have been made from almost any timber, but in fact is Australian rosewood. I chose

Photo 1 *Butterfly Bowl,* rosewood, 350mm 13 ¾" W.

comes naturally

this wood because it is light, but strong and easily carved. The walls needed to be thin so the carved-through insect and plants would seem fragile.

Photo 2 is another example of 'form over features'. The wood is masur birch and the form nicely shows the grain. But it could have been made from another timber without altering the design in any way.

When we are seriously influenced by the found qualities of the piece of wood we can go to the other extreme. **Photo 3** shows a piece I hardly turned at all. It's a bunya pine knot which had been grub-eaten while still in the tree.

The sapwood is soft and easily devoured, but the heartwood is very hard and remained intact. After the sapwood had been almost completely consumed, the knot fell out of the tree, to be found on the forest floor.

It so resembled a plumb bob that I minimally turned each end and designed a metal stand for it. It is titled *It All Depends,* which is my response when people ask what it means.

A friend in Finland recently sent me another piece of masur birch which had the most extraordinary texture on the outside. It would have been criminal to turn it off, so I decided any work I would do had to avoid the outside entirely.

Photo 4 shows the result — a container where the only interesting turned feature is the bead which defines the lip.

My favourite type of turning is hollow forms which incorporate natural holes and faults. The holes allow intriguing peep views inside, and I find people

▶

Photo 2 *Vase,* masur birch, 170mm 6 ¾" H.

Photo 3 *It All Depends,* bunya pine and iron, 950mm 37 ⅜" H.

Photo 4 *Container,* masur birch, 150mm 6" H.

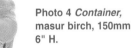

TERRY MARTIN

Terry Martin was born in Melbourne in 1947. A graduate of University of South Australia, and University of New England, he has had a satisfying and adventurous life travelling the world in various capacities, including Stage Manager of the Royal Opera House, Covent Garden, Ski Patrol in Austria, geological exploration in the Pacific Islands and Migrant Education in Australia. A growing appreciation of fine craft work was heightened by several years spent in Japan and when Terry returned to Australia he decided to pursue his interest in woodcraft.
Terry believes that woodturning allows use of limited timber resources for maximum effect. Much of the wood he uses is recycled, such as fence posts or railway sleepers. Influenced by Japanese ceramics and other crafts, he believes that the natural faults of the timber should be allowed to remain to enhance the work he does on the wood.

are more fascinated by these pieces than hollow forms with complete walls.

Perhaps it convinces them the pieces really are hollow, or it allows them to see that the walls are as thin as the weight of the piece suggests. The holes actually make hollowing easier because the shavings can escape during cutting and wall thickness can be visually confirmed.

Photo 5 is a hollow form in coolibah burl (burr) which has three holes more or less symmetrically placed around the outside. This was, of course, not pure chance.

The burl had to be chosen for this feature and the positioning of the wood on the lathe is crucial, as clumsy placement of the holes completely spoils the effect.

This is a case where the wood features and the imposed form have to enhance each other. **Photo 6**, a hollow form in sandalwood, is another example of the same effect.

SHAPE

Frequently, the rim of a turned wooden vessel is the defining feature which formalises the shape. But the natural-edged vessel has been a popular alternative for many years. In **Photo 7** you can see a hollow form I made from a blood-wood burl (burr).

The shape is smooth and ovoid, but it ends in the jagged rim of the natural exterior. I blackened this rim to emphasise the contrast and, again, the viewer is immediately tempted to see what is inside. The pair of vessels in **Photo 8**

also feature the natural exterior of the tree.

Recently, I was commissioned to turn a series of vessels for an exhibition of ikebana, or flower-arranging, in Japan. The ikebana artist wanted to use Australian plants and requested the vessels reflected the "robust qualities of Australian nature".

I produced a set of bowls which contrast the formality of the bowl shape with the chipped and weathered exterior of the tree trunk, leaving as much of the natural texture as I could.

Photo 9 shows one of these bowls produced from an old red gum log which had been laying in the bush for nearly 50 years.

If I was asked which pieces I have enjoyed turning most over recent years, all of these would be high on the list. Turning timber like this is an adventure, and the results can be unpredictable, not to say disastrous.

But it's fun to incorporate quirks of nature into your turnings, and I often say some of my best work is done by the grubs!

Of course basic design must be good, but what constitutes good design will always be a matter of opinion.

It doesn't hurt to break the rules. In fact I would go further and say, safety considerations aside, the only rule is there are no rules. ●

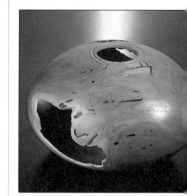

Photo 5 *Hollow Form,* coolibah, 170mm 6 ¾" H.

'**My** favourite type of turning is hollow forms which incorporate natural holes and faults'.
'It's fun to incorporate quirks of nature into your work, and I often say some of my best work is done by grubs!'

Photo 9 *Ikebana Bowl*, red gum, 160mm 6 ¼" H.

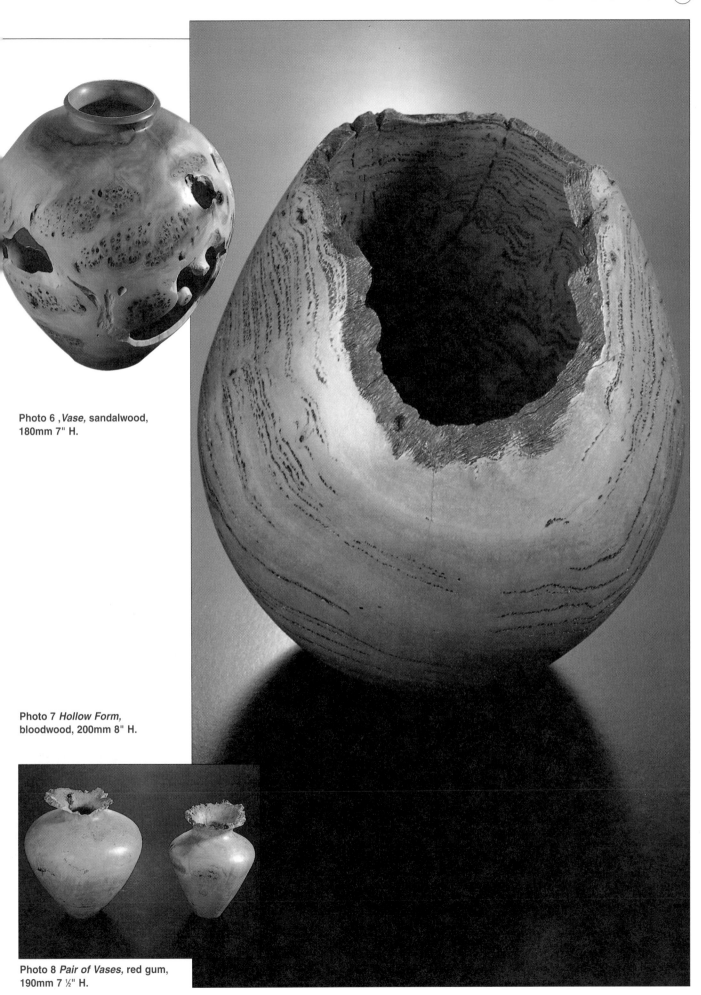

Photo 6 , *Vase,* sandalwood,
180mm 7" H.

Photo 7 *Hollow Form,*
bloodwood, 200mm 8" H.

Photo 8 *Pair of Vases,* red gum,
190mm 7 ½" H.

"Like a Potter's Vessel"

GEOFF HEATH

How, wondered the author, would it be possible to produce a hollow vessel with an internal finish equal to the external one without resorting to the use of expensive tools? This project describes his solution.

Geoff Heath is a self-taught turner who has been improving his skills since he took up the craft as a hobby in 1975.

He began woodturning as a relaxation from his job as Chief Structural Engineer at the Woodford factory of British Aerospace, and since he retired in 1988 he has been able to spend more time at his hobby. However, it still has to compete with his other interests of choral singing, attending an art class, committee work for his local residents' association, and domestic chores including gardening.

Geoff has always been interested in ingenious ways of solving problems, especially those involving lateral thinking. He uses the nom-de-plume "Skew" as the setter of the prize crossword in *Woodturning*, since he believes that crossword compilers need to think in a skewed fashion!

Geoff is a founder member of the High Peak Woodturners. He is also a Chartered Engineer, a Fellow of the Institution of Mechanical Engineers, and a Fellow of the Royal Aeronautical Society.

Perhaps it was because I belong to our local choral society that the words of the psalmist which appear in Handel's *Messiah* ('Thou shalt dash them in pieces like a potter's vessel') leapt to mind as I walked round an exhibition of woodturning. Not that I had any such destructive desires; it was the final phrase 'like a potter's vessel' that came to my lips, for the turner has much in common with the potter, and many of the artefacts we turners produce are wooden replicas of those which come off the potter's wheel.

The items which intrigued me most were the hollow vessels. I can't call them 'pots' for obvious reasons, and I can't think of another word to describe them. Fellow-turners will know what I mean — roughly spherical in shape, they have a small opening at the top through which the turner has poked about with a fancy tool to remove the inside. Often the vessel features 'natural' or 'man-made' apertures through

which the admiring public can see just how thin the wall is. The interior is sometimes painted matt black or even — what sacrilege! — scorched with a blow-lamp. To my cynical mind, such treatment suggests that the turner was not happy with the internal surface finish, and did his best to hide it.

'Wild'

So I set myself the problem: how could I produce such a vessel without resorting to expensive tools, and with an internal finish as good as the external one? The obvious answer was to make the vessel in two halves, each half being like a bowl. Ah, yes, but how was I to disguise the join? Here the solution was to inlay an equatorial band of contrasting wood alongside the join, so that the eye would not notice the interruption to the basic grain pattern. This device would be more effective, I reasoned, if the grain were as 'wild' as possible, thus making its convolutions even harder to trace from one side of the band to the other.

I was fortunate in having a large board of elm in stock; this was 75mm 3″ thick and around 380mm 15″ wide, with one square edge. The bowls I had already turned from this wood were full of burrs, round which the grain wandered in a delightful fashion. Here was the ideal wood from which to make my vessel.

I started by cutting out two 150mm 6″ square blocks which lay alongside each other near the waney edge. I thus arranged for the proportions of sapwood and heartwood to be roughly the same in each block, and for the two pieces to be 'bookmatched' on one face (Fig 1). The blocks were labelled 'top' and 'bottom' to avoid any subsequent confusion. These preliminary steps ensured that the top of the vessel would be a reasonable 'mirror image' of the bottom. Circular blanks were then bandsawed from the blocks (Fig 2).

Fig 1
Two square blocks, 'book-matched' on the top face, after cutting from the burr elm board

Fig 2
Turning blanks cut from the two blocks. The 'mirror image' effect is clearly shown

Upper Half

With this initial work completed, it was time to get on with the interesting part — turning. I started with the upper half; this was mounted on the faceplate with four screws into the top face (Fig 3). It was important that the screws did not go in too deep, and the pitch circle of the screws had to be big enough to leave sufficient material for the wide lip which was to surround the neck. I had intended to insert a disc of hardboard between the faceplate and the workpiece. This would have served two functions: reducing the penetration of the screws, and preventing the saw-tooth bit (with which I drilled the hole for the throat) from hitting the faceplate. In the event, I forgot it!

Fig 3
The top of the vessel mounted for turning. Care had to be taken in choosing the pitch circle diameter of the screws in the faceplate

Fig 4
The neck and lip area reduced to the diameter of the faceplate

The wood surrounding the faceplate was then cut back with a parting-off tool to leave a disc about 20mm ¾″ thick with the same diameter as the faceplate itself (Fig 4), the diameter later being reduced still further in the region of the neck. The outside of the top was then roughly turned to shape

Fig 5
The outside of the top roughed out, with further reduction in diameter of the neck

(Fig 5). The free end was cleaned up, and the hollowing-out of the top commenced with a bowl-turning gouge. Before the wall got too thin, the rebate for the joining of the two halves

was cut with the parting-off tool, and a 1″ hole drilled through the top (Fig 6) with the

Fig 6
The top hollowed out, showing the rebate for the joint with the lower half of the vessel, and the hole drilled for the throat

saw-tooth bit held in a chuck in the tailstock.

The inside of the top was now finished, using various scrapers, abrasive papers of diminishing grit size, sanding sealer, Danish oil and wax polish (Fig 7). I found it necessary to support the workpiece with my left hand whilst I applied the scraper with the right in order to reduce 'tool chatter' as the wall thickness was reduced to about 6mm ¼″.

Now the top was removed from the lathe and unscrewed from the faceplate. It had been my original intention to finish the outside of the neck and the lip when the two halves were glued together but, fearing that the overhang from the chuck would be too great, I decided to finish these areas completely before

Fig 8
The disc of scrap wood used for mounting the top, showing the rebate on the rim

making the base. Accordingly, I mounted a disc of scrap wood on the faceplate, turned a rebate into it to match the one in the top (Fig 8), and pressed the top into position, securing it with masking tape. The neck and lip were now finished completely (Fig 9), but I left the finishing of the rest of the top until it was mated with the base.

Fig 9
The top mounted on the disc, with the neck area completely finished. Note the use of masking tape to strap the workpiece in place

Fig 7
The inside of the top finished and polished. Note the radius at the entry to the throat

Fig 10
The base mounted on the faceplate, showing the finished base and the recess for the expanding chuck. The central boss and the concentric ring are purely decorative, and are the author's 'trademark'

Fig 11
The base showing the recess for the inlay alongside the rebate for the joint

The Base

Then it was time to start the base, which was a straight-forward piece of bowl-turning. The workpiece was first screwed to the faceplate to enable the outside to be roughed out, and a recess was cut into the bottom for an expanding chuck. The recess and the surrounding area were then sanded, oiled and polished (Fig 10), after which the base was transferred from the faceplate to the chuck, where it remained until the vessel was entirely finished.

The next step was to cut a rebate around the rim of the base to mate with the one in the top, with a shallower rebate about 20mm ¾" wide just below it for the inlay (Fig 11). The inlay was cut from a piece of beech by slicing thin strips across the grain with the bandsaw. These were sufficiently flexible to accept being bent to the required curvature without the need to steam them, and were glued into place and held with rubber bands until the PVA adhesive had set (Fig 12).

Fig 12
The inlay glued in place, retained by rubber bands

Now the inside of the base was hollowed out with a bowl gouge, taking the precaution of cutting 'anti-skid' grooves into the face to prevent the gouge from skating sideways and chipping the edge (Fig 13). The internal

Fig 13
The base ready for hollowing-out. Note the inlay and the 'anti-skid' grooves in the face

surface was scraped to a good finish, sanded, oiled and polished. Adhesive was then applied to the joint, and the two halves were glued together, the tailstock being used to apply pressure via a revolving centre until the glue had set. A block of soft foam from a worn-out scouring pad was used to protect the lip from damage during this operation (Fig 14).

The revolving centre and foam pad were left in place while the outside of the vessel (including the inlay) was reduced to its final thickness with a scraper, followed by the usual sanding, oiling and waxing. The vessel was now complete (Fig 15), and was removed from the lathe (Fig 16).

Fig 14
The top mated with the base. Note the foam pad between the revolving centre and the neck, used to avoid bruising the lip when pressure was applied via the tailstock

Fig 15
The finished vessel, ready for removal from the lathe

Fig 16
'Like a potter's vessel'

Natural Cavities

Although I had achieved my aim of producing a thin-walled vessel with a good inside finish, I was aware that only I knew what the inside looked like. One could peer in through the throat but, unless some form of lighting was introduced, the interior was too dark to examine. What were needed as starting-points were two blocks of wood with natural cavities which would subsequently become holes through the walls of the finished vessel.

I therefore went back to my burr elm board, and cut two more blocks — not from adjacent locations, but chosen for their natural features. The one for the base had a large piece of enclosed bark, while the one for the top was cut so as to include the waney edge of the board (Fig 17). A second vessel was made (Figs 18, 19, 20), using exactly the same procedure as that described above, but with a narrower (12mm ½″) throat and a smaller lip. This time, I remembered the protective disc between the faceplate and the workpiece!

Expanding Collets

I was also more daring in the choice of chuck, using 45mm 1¾″ expanding collets instead

Fig 17
The second pair of blanks, showing the natural features which became holes in the finished vessel

Fig 18
The top of the second vessel partly turned. The presence of the natural cavity meant that only three of the four faceplate screw-holes could be used. Note the protective disc of hardboard between the faceplate and the workpiece

of 70mm 2¾″. The corresponding reduction in the diameter of the recess in the base should have enabled me to make the vessel more spherical

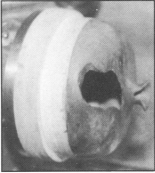

Fig 19
The top nearly finished. Note the natural cutaway in the lip, the hole through the wall and the masking tape strapping

Fig 20
The base showing the hole produced by the fall-out of the enclosed bark. The inlay and the rebate for the joint can also be seen

but, in the event, the need to make a feature of the hole from the enclosed bark dictated a shape even more cylindrical than the first effort (Fig 21).

Fig 21
The second vessel ready for removal from the lathe. The inlay had to be cut away locally to reveal the full extent of the natural hole in the base

However, a comparison of the two vessels (Fig 22) shows that the second one is much more interesting. The inlay is of Sonokeling rosewood, which is a dark greeny-purple colour, contrasting less markedly with the elm than did the beech. The two irregular holes in the top and bottom enable the interior to be viewed without difficulty, and even the neck is partly cut away. At this stage I felt that my objective had been achieved; I had not used any tools other than those found in an average turner's tool rack, and I had produced a hollow vessel with a narrow neck, thin walls and a polished interior. ∎

Fig 22
The two vessels compared

Dennis Elliott was born in London, England, in 1950. He married his American wife Iona in 1972 and has been a resident of the US (currently living in Sherman, Connecticut) since 1975. He is both a musician and woodturner by profession.

Dennis started turning wood in 1972 and is basically self taught. For the last few years he has been concentrating mainly on large burlwood vessels and wall sculptures with frequent use of sandblasting and carving techniques. His works can be found in major corporate and private collections.

Among the awards he has received are 'Honoraria' Texas Fine Arts Association's New American Talent 1988; 'Award of Distinction' The Pennsylvania State University, Crafts 22; 'Best in Wood Award' The Octagon Center for the Arts, Ames, Iowa 1989; 'Certificate of Excellence in Wood' Art Horizons — a leading International Art Competition, New York; and '1991 Master Craftsman Honor' The Society of Connecticut Craftsmen.

He is co-founder of the Nutmeg Woodturners' League and a founding member of the American Association of Woodturners.

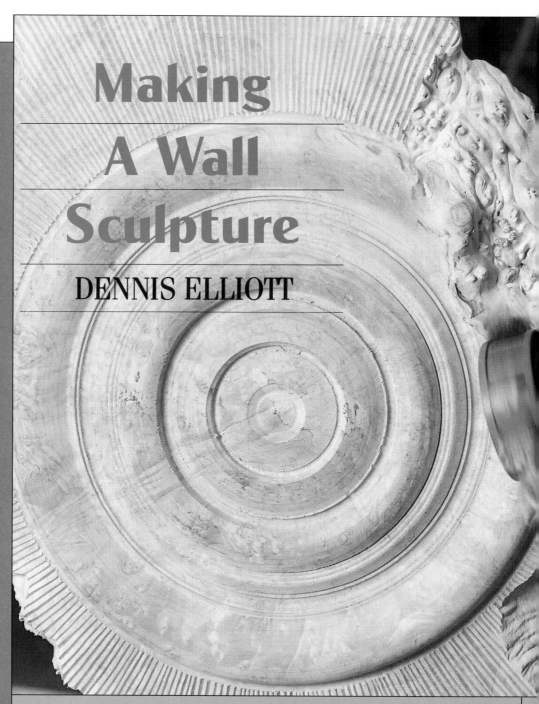

Making A Wall Sculpture

DENNIS ELLIOTT

'Just let the imagination run wild. Remember, this is controlled mayhem.'

Making these wall pieces evolved from the humble platter. I get platter material delivered in slabs 75mm 3″ thick and any diameter from my usual supplier in Oregon on the west coast of the United States (which is somewhat unfortunate as I live on the east Coast). It is maple burl and is quite dry when it arrives and usually very stable. These slabs come in all sorts of shapes and sizes and sometimes

with one or two straight edges from chainsaw cuts. My normal procedure would be to cut out a circle and make a platter. Well, when this particular shipment arrived, several of the slabs were completely surrounded by the natural surface of the burl, as if cut from a very large and fairly symmetrical burl, which of course they were. I must admit I don't think I would have the heart to do that myself, but I

later found out that this shipment was originally destined for a veneer company in Japan. As is much of our wood, it seems! Well there's no way I'm now going to mark out a circle, cut out a disc, and throw away the natural edge of this stuff just to make a platter, is there? No! How about something naturally sculptural, surrounding a nice smooth platter, I thought.

I've seen similar works like this before, so I can claim little originality here, but the pieces I've seen have always had a flat area on the edge somewhere.

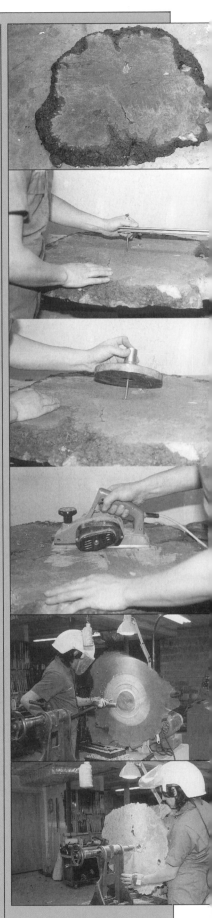

Big leaf maple burl, pink alabaster, African blackwood and metal.
50mm 2″ H x 685mm 27″ W x 815mm 32″ L.
Selected for the International Lathe-Turned Objects Challenge IV Exhibition.

it took a matter of moments to think of the potential that existed in the remaining slabs!

Picture this . . .

You are the worst turner on the planet and platters are your least successful endeavour to date. They exhibit every fault possible, i.e. peaks, valleys, rough surface, spiral cuts, burn marks, a few holes and a little handwork thrown in for good measure. Magnify all those faults ten thousand times, then learn how to cut them all cleanly, and you should get an idea of the content of these pieces . . . sort of controlled mayhem! The wood becomes your canvas and a mirror of your mind! AGGGGGHHHHHHH.

I hate explaining why I make things, but I like explaining how! Let's take a look at one of these slabs, and what we want from it.

This one measures 34″ x 29″ (850mm x 725mm) and I want the face to be the surface that has the natural burl edge sloping back to the wall (Photo 1). (Platters are the opposite so you can pick them up.)

Finding Centre

The first thing I want to find is the centre, or rather the point of visual balance. To do this I just play around with the compass until I draw a circle that relates to the natural edge. I mark this centre with a tap on the point of the compass (Photo 2) and locate my faceplate (Photo 3). If it doesn't sit flat. I'll plane it true (Photo 4). I can now put it on the lathe and true up the base (Photo 5, wall side). I then run up my tailstock and mark the centre (Photo 6). I can now take off the faceplate, knowing that my new centre point is exactly opposite on the other side.

This was an opportunity for me to make something special.

Make them I did. Very successful they were, but I was getting to the bottom of the pile now and, although they still had the natural edge, they had problems. One was bark inclusions, which, if not loose now, soon will be and would probably result in holes or canyons in the surface. I think, even on a semifunctional platter, that is undesirable. The second problem was size. I personally think a 915mm 36″ platter is a bit overkill and these wouldn't be in proportion now, more like 890mm 35″ x 635mm 25″.

Now the aforementioned 'platters', when fulfilling their 'function' in the middle of the dining room table, did look big and beautiful. But what do you do when you want to use the table? Put it on the floor? No! I include some form of keyhole hanger on the back, either a routed one or a solid brass recessed one. Note that it should not be one that is secured to the wood with those little brass nails! Can you imagine a 10lb object landing on your bowling trophy!

We are now into wall pieces, and

From top to bottom
Photos 1, 2, 3, 4, 5, 6.

Photo 7

Photo 8

Photo 9

These screwholes on the face side will be removed by a deep cut or recess (Photos 7 & 8). If I were to use the same faceplate on the back, the screws would be on the same line and quite possibly touched by the turning tool. I'll use a larger one and get the screws out into an area that will be one of our peaks on the face (Photo 9).

The bar in the faceplate in photo 9 is just an aluminium dowel, threaded to fit the faceplate. It has a hole down its centre, to accept a pointed rod. What this does is reduce the large hole in the faceplate to a small point which can locate in the hole made by the tailstock.

Grooves

Once back on the lathe, I start to thin out, and taper down the area outside the first round section (Photo 10). I then go in with a small ¼″ (6mm) round nose scraper (or even a parting tool will do) to deeply define and visually separate these two areas. The outer tapered area will be carved with a reciprocating gouge (Photo 11) to create tight 'V' grooves that will radiate outward and draw the eye towards the centre.

The central area is turned with regular turning techniques and I won't even try to describe it. Just let the imagination run wild. But keep in mind that, because of the complex nature, it can be tricky to sand. I try to cut every detail with sharp gouges aiming for clean, precise lines. Remember, this is *controlled mayhem!*

Make no mistake about this type of work, it can be dangerous. If I'm feeling at all anxious or nervous about anything, I will not make these pieces.

It also takes good equipment and I always wear face and head protection (Photo 12). In fact, I usually call the local hospital emergency room to see if they are busy before I start! ONLY KIDDING! ■

The finished piece. Now in the collection of Anitra Peebles Skeen.
Big leaf maple burl.
50mm 2″ H x 725mm 29″ W x 850mm 34″ L

Photo 10

Photo 11

Photo 12

Index

Titles available from
Guild of Master Craftsman Publications

Books

Carving Birds and Beasts	GMC Publications
Practical Tips for Turners & Carvers	GMC Publications
Practical Tips for Woodturners	GMC Publications
Useful Woodturning Projects	GMC Publications
Woodturning Techniques	GMC Publications
Woodworkers' Career and Educational Source Book	GMC Publications
Woodworkers' Courses & Source Book	GMC Publications
Woodworking Crafts Annual	GMC Publications
Woodworking Plans and Projects	GMC Publications
40 More Woodworking Plans and Projects	GMC Publications
Green Woodwork	Mike Abbott
Easy to Make Dolls' House Accessories	Andrea Barham
Making Little Boxes from Wood	John Bennett
Woodturning Masterclass	Tony Boase
Furniture Restoration and Repair for Beginners	Kevin Jan Bonner
Woodturning Jewellery	Hilary Bowen
The Incredible Router	Jeremy Broun
Electric Woodwork	Jeremy Broun
Woodcarving: A Complete Course	Ron Butterfield
Making Fine Furniture: Projects	Tom Darby
Restoring Rocking Horses	Clive Green & Anthony Dew
Heraldic Miniature Knights	Peter Greenhill
Make Your Own Dolls' House Furniture	Maurice Harper
Seat Weaving (Practical Crafts)	Ricky Holdstock
Multi-centre Woodturning	Ray Hopper
Complete Woodfinishing	Ian Hosker
Woodturning: A Source Book of Shapes	John Hunnex
Making Shaker Furniture	Barry Jackson
Upholstery: A Complete Course	David James
Upholstery Techniques and Projects	David James
The Upholsterer's Pocket Reference Book	David James
Designing and Making Wooden Toys	Terry Kelly
Making Dolls' House Furniture	Patricia King
Making Victorian Dolls' House Furniture	Patricia King
Making and Modifying Woodworking Tools	Jim Kingshott
The Workshop	Jim Kingshott
Sharpening: The Complete Guide	Jim Kingshott
Turning Wooden Toys	Terry Lawrence
Making Board, Peg and Dice Games	Jeff & Jennie Loader
Making Wooden Toys and Games	Jeff & Jennie Loader
Bert Marsh: Woodturner	Bert Marsh
The Complete Dolls' House Book	Jean Nisbett
The Secrets of the Dolls' House Makers	Jean Nisbett

Wildfowl Carving: Volume 1	Jim Pearce
Make Money from Woodturning	Ann & Bob Phillips
Guide to Marketing	Jack Pigden
The Complete Pyrography	Stephen Poole
Woodcarving Tools, Materials and Equipment	Chris Pye
Carving on Turning	Chris Pye
Making Tudor Dolls' Houses	Derek Rowbottom
Making Georgian Dolls' Houses	Derek Rowbottom
Making Period Dolls' House Furniture	Derek & Sheila Rowbottom
Woodturning: A Foundation Course	Keith Rowley
Turning Miniatures in Wood	John Sainsbury
Pleasure and Profit from Woodturning	Reg Sherwin
Making Unusual Miniatures	Graham Spalding
Woodturning Wizardry	David Springett
Adventures in Woodturning	David Springett
Furniture Projects	Rod Wales
Decorative Woodcarving	Jeremy Williams

Videos

Dennis White Teaches Woodturning:
  Part 1 Turning Between Centres
  Part 2 Turning Bowls
  Part 3 Boxes, Goblets and Screw Threads
  Part 4 Novelties and Projects
  Part 5 Classic Profiles
  Part 6 Twists and Advanced Turning
John Jordan Bowl Turning
John Jordan Hollow Turning
Jim Kingshott Sharpening the Professional Way
Jim Kingshott Sharpening Turning and Carving Tools
Ray Gonzalez Carving a Figure: The Female Form
David James The Traditional Upholstery Workshop:
  Part I: Drop-in and Pinstuffed Seats
  Part II: Stuffover Upholstery

GMC Publications regularly produces new books and videos on a wide range of woodworking and craft subjects, and an increasing number of specialist magazines, all available on subscription:

Magazines

WOODTURNING   WOODCARVING   BUSINESSMATTERS

All these publications are available through bookshops and newsagents, or may be ordered by post from the publishers at Castle Place, 166 High Street, Lewes, East Sussex BN7 1XU, telephone (01273) 477374, fax (01273) 478606.
Credit card orders are accepted.

PLEASE WRITE OR PHONE FOR A FREE CATALOGUE